Robby's Raiders

A History of Bellefonte High School

Baseball 1964-1981

By Ralph Gray

2018

Cover:
A Shawnee Warrior,
Native of the Bellefonte Area of Pennsylvania.

Please direct all correspondence and book orders to:

Ralph Gray
P.O. Box 408
Millheim, PA 16854

Phone: 814-349-5740

Email: RNK12161@verizon.net

Table of Contents

Introduction…………………………………………………………..Page   1

Some Bellefonte Baseball History Prior to 1964…………………………..Page   2

Baseball at the Grange Fair……………………………………… . Page   9

Donald Harpster Robinson…………………………………………Page   22

Robby at Penn State…………………………………………..Page   23

Robby in the County League……………………………………..Page   29

Robby—A Winning Baseball Coach……………………………….Page   31

The Baseball Seasons:

1964…………………………………………………..Page   34

1965…………………………………………………..Page   46

1966…………………………………………………..Page   49

1967…………………………………………………..Page   58

1968…………………………………………………..Page   66

1969…………………………………………………..Page   78

1970…………………………………………………..Page   81

1971…………………………………………………..Page   83

1972…………………………………………………..Page   85

1973…………………………………………………..Page   95

Table of Contents—cont.

1974...Page 104

1975...Page 106

1976..Page 108

1977...Page 114

Denny Leathers...Page 120

1978...Page 128

1979...Page 130

1980...Page 133

1981...Page 137

A Pair of Aces.. Page 139

Robby's 18-year Record.. ..Page 140

Bellefonte Athletics 1964-81...Page 141

Epilogue...Page 142

About The Author...Page 143

Acknowledgements and Bibliography......................................Page 144

Index..Page 145

Introduction

The 1963 Bellefonte Baseball Team was loaded with talent led by pitcher and shortstop Denny Leathers, a member of the Centre County Sports Hall of Fame, a former professional baseball player and a successful head coach of the Bellefonte Red Raider High School Baseball Program.

Coached by Forest Benford and assistant Ralph Dale, the 1963 squad, which was composed mainly of the 1958 Pennsylvania State Little League Championship Team and the 1961 Pennsylvania State Babe Ruth Championship Team, started the season with a 4-0 record in the Central Penn League.

However, the Raiders lost three of the next four games and ended the season in a tie with State College, resulting in a playoff game for the league title, which was won by State College, 2-1. Benford and Dale resigned after the 1963 season.

Former Penn State baseball star Don Robinson from Port Matilda, Pa.; was hired to coach the Red Raiders in 1964. Also hired was assistant coach Ralph Gray, a former American Legion Baseball All-Star from Barnesboro, in Cambria County. Robinson and Gray were teachers in the Bellefonte school system.

The new Raider coaches had not known each other prior to their hiring; but worked well together and formed a friendship that lasts to this day. In 1964 Gray lived in an apartment on South Spring Street in Bellefonte; and Robinson lived in a mobile home in Port Matilda. When Gray moved to East End in Bellefonte in 1968, the Robinsons moved into the apartment formerly occupied by the Grays.

Robinson later bought a house on Centre Street in East End which bordered the Gray property; and the pair became neighbors, as well.

This book is about Don Robinson, the teams he coached from 1964 to 1981, and the impact he had on the Bellefonte High School baseball program.

Ralph Gray　　　　　　　　**Don Robinson**

Some Bellefonte Baseball History Prior to 1964

1911—The Bellefonte Academy defeated the Bellefonte H.S. Baseball Team.

Bellefonte's East Bishop Street circa 1912

In those days Bellefonte High School played its baseball games on the grounds of the Bellefonte Academy's eight-acre athletic complex, the current site of Rainbow Village. The complex was surrounded by a board fence and consisted of a football-baseball field, a cinder track, a large swimming pool, and tennis courts.

The Bellefonte Community Baseball Field, the Athletic Field (football stadium), and the Bellefonte Senior High School were eventually built across the street from the Beaver Farm on the former Bellefonte Airfield.

1919—Bellefonte High fielded a baseball team.

The 1919 Major League Baseball season is best remembered for the Black Sox Scandal, in which the Chicago White Sox threw (purposely lost) the World Series to the Cincinnati Reds 5-3, in order to illegally gain money from gambling.

BASE BALL

Last year Bellefonte High was represented on the diamond. This year we are exceptionately fortunate in having considerable material, for all varsity men, except two of last years team, are in school this year and will be put for their positions.

Proper support will place Bellefonte High's name in the Hall of Base Ball Fame. Help all you can and keep up the honor of B. H. S. in sports.

The Base-Ball Schedule for this season is as follows:

April 23 Bellefonte vs. Lock Haven Normal (at Lock Haven).
April 24 Bellefonte vs. State College High (at Bellefonte).
May 1 Bellefonte vs. Huntingdon High (at Huntingdon).
May 4 Bellefonte vs. State College High (at State College).
May 14 Bellefonte vs. Lock Haven Normal (at Bellefonte).
Open dates—May 8 and 15.

On April 22, the baseball season of Bellefonte High School was opened with the Lock Haven Normal School as an opponent. Some of the candidates for the team had been members of the basket ball squad; these boys were ordered to rest for a few days to be in condition for baseball. For several days the rainy weather prevented them from practicing, so that when the boys went to Lock Haven they had very little practice.

The boys put up a good game and it surely would have been better if they could have had some batting practice. The Lock Haven team could score not more than one run in each inning, before our boys found themselves. The final score was 7-0.

OUR FIRST VICTORY

The second game of the season was with State College High at Bellefonte. Owing to the high wind the weather conditions were unfavorable for a good game.

At the beginning of the game the outcome looked bad for our boys, but in the fourth inning they succeeded in taking the lead from their opponents, and kept it until the end of the game, the final score being 19-4.

This game gives us a more convincing evidence that our baseball season of 1920 will be a successful one.

Line Up for State College Game.

P. Johnson, c............................Wagner, c.
T. Mensch, p............................Roundtree, c.
H. Johnston, s. s............................Campbell, s. s.
M. Wetzel, f. b............................Robb, f. b.
W. Kline, s. b............................Stephens, s. b.
N. Robb, t. b............................Light, t. b.
W. Hugg, l. f............................Scott, l. f.
B. Tingue, c. f............................Kennedy, l. f.
D. Bullock, r. f............................Witmer, r. f.

Umpires—Bases, Buchannan; Strikes, Kaplan.

Substitutions—Rider for Bullock, Thompson for Tingue, Witmer for Wagner, Shuey ofr Witmer, Galbraith for Roundtree.

The schedule for the rest of the season is as follows:

May 1 Huntingdon High at Huntingdon.
May 4 State College High at State.
May 14 Lock Haven Normal at Bellefonte.

1920 BASEBALL SEASON. Lineup on the left is Bellefonte.

1921

The interest in baseball was running high in Bellefonte High School as a result of the inter-class league which was newly organized in 1921 to decide the class championship as well as to give Coach Earl K. Stock a line on the material for the varsity baseball team.

The first league game was played between the seniors and the sophomores, the former easily winning, 11-1.

In the next game, the juniors defeated the freshmen, 8-4.

The sophomores easily defeated the freshmen 11-3, thus putting the freshmen in last place.

In a closely contested game. the seniors went into first place by defeating the juniors, 3-0.

The league standings were as follows with two games yet to play:

Inter-Class League

	Won	Lost	Pct.
SENIORS	2	0	1.000
JUNIORS	1	1	.500
SOPHOMORES	1	1	.500
FRESHMEN	0	2	.000

With the class games finished, Coach Stock picked a varsity team from the best players on the different teams to play the games on the schedule which was being made by Manager Warren "Ty" Cobb.

A practice game was played with Centre Hall High School on April 16. The Bellefonte High School Team came out victorious, 8-7.

With the varsity material back from the 1920 team and promising new material, a winning team was expected in the 1921 season.

Picture at left:

Hughes Field in Bellefonte on East Bishop Street where the high school team played until 1937.

It was the home field of the Bellefonte Academy Baseball Team from 1910 to 1932. It is now the site of Rainbow Village.

1921 Bellefonte High School Baseball Team

That baseball was a howling success in 1921 is clearly shown by the fact that out of six starts, five victories were recorded. Lock Haven had the honor of beating Bellefonte on their field.

Judging from all indications, the 1922 team was expected to surpass the record made on the diamond the previous year.

On account of Coach Stock being so busy with his school responsibilities and coaching track, William "Essig" Kline became the new baseball coach. Essig knew baseball and had succeeded in developing a winning team, for in the two early games, Bellefonte came out victorious. The first, a practice game with Pleasant Gap, ended in the second inning with the score at 25-0; the second with Mill Hall, closed with Bellefonte on the long end of a 14-8 score.

From the showing made by the team in those two games, victories were predicted in the bigger games on the schedule that Manager Lyons was working on.

1923 Bellefonte High School Baseball Team

The 1923 baseball team was the best team that Bellefonte High School had fielded for some time. The team came out the victor in all the games except two—tying one with Lock Haven and losing one to State College High on their field. They were Bellefonte's only rivals—splitting the two games played.

When Lock Haven played at Bellefonte, it rained; but the home team came out on top. At Lock Haven, the boys played the best game of the season. The score was 3-3 after eleven innings, and the game ended on account of darkness.

In the two games with Centre Hall, Bellefonte proved to be the victor; and in the Philipsburg game at Philipsburg, Bellefonte won without much trouble.

1923 Penn State Baseball Team: First Row, L-R: Merz, Fink, Loetiler. Bedenk, Capt. Koehler, Palm, Wise, Reed, Fortna. **Row 2:** Coach Bezdek, Kelley, Shutt, Miller, Black, Fixter, Longhurst, Hollobaugh, Malin, Manager Musser.

The Baseball Team

Dorworth, Stere, Tice, Schenck, McCullough, Harvey, Martin, Mr. Gilston,
Clark, Emel, Harshberger, Malone, Johnson,
Robb   Carpeneto

BASEBALL SCHEDULE 1924

*April 16.	Centre Hall High School	4	B. H. S.	2
*April 25.	Gregg Township Vocational School	5	B. H. S.	10
April 28.	Centre Hall High School	9	B. H. S.	7
*May 2.	State College High School	10	B. H. S.	15
May 6.	Gregg Township Vocational School	2	B. H. S.	15
*May 7.	Lock Haven High School	8	B. H. S.	4
May 15.	Philipsburg High School	4	B. H. S.	5
May 20.	Lock Haven High School	11	B. H. S.	0
May 22.	State College High School	1	B. H. S.	6
June 3.	Millheim High School	7	B. H. S.	1

*Games away.

Samuel Harshberger captained the 1924 team.

7

1926—After the 1926 season, Bellefonte High dropped baseball as an interscholastic sport.

1926—Seniors on the Bellefonte High School Baseball Team: Malcolm W. Wagner, James B. McCullough, Charles A. Mensch, Franklin G. Malone, and Joseph Herman. Malone played four years for Bellefonte High.

Bellefonte High School in 1926 at the corner of West Linn And North Allegheny Streets.

1926 Bellefonte player

Above: Bellefonte baseball practice is snowed out in 1926.

At right: Bellefonte baseball player at the high school.

Baseball at the Grange Fair

Many years ago, there was a baseball diamond in the northeast corner of the Grange Fair Grounds. In the photo at the left, the ball field is in the lower left corner. A popular Fair attraction was the Championship Tournament of the Centre County League that took place there. For example, on Tuesday, August 30, 1932 (Junior Day), there was a ball game scheduled between Howard and Pleasant Gap at 3 p.m. Baseball games used to be an aspect of entertainment at the Fair, e.g., on Wednesday, August 31, 1932 (Education Day), a game was scheduled between Pine Grove Mills and the Colored Giants of Mount Union.

The wildest and perhaps the longest game ever played in Centre County baseball history occurred at Grange Park on August 21, 1927.

Playing before a huge crowd, Centre Hall and Grass Flat, tied at 1-1, battled for 19 innings before the team captains and umpire Ed Keichline decided to end the deadlock. Both teams were weary; and since neither team wanted to lose, the decision to call the game was satisfactory to all the players.

Pitchers Russ Cable of Centre Hall and Stiney Lawrence of Grass Flat both pitched the entire game and neither man issued a base on balls. Cable struck out 14 while Lawrence fanned 13. Both runs were unearned; and the errors that caused them were the only two miscues in the entire game.

Centre Hall had a scoring opportunity in the 10th inning with one out and George Goodhart on third. Wim Stover hit a grounder to the second baseman; but on the throw Goodhart was dead on arrival at the plate.

In the 16th inning, Ran Keller of Centre Hall retired the side by catching all three fly balls. Albert Emery made several star catches in center field for Centre Hall. A strikeout by Centre Hall's Harry Gross was the final "out" in the 19th.

Centre Hall first baseman Newton "Doc" Crawford recorded 29 putouts without an error, while third baseman Goodhart and shortstop Ralph Martz combined for 15 assists.

Centre Hall lineup: Goodhart, Martz, Stover, Crawford, Cable, Keller, H. Gross, A. Emery, Reiber, Fetterolf. Grass Flat lineup: B. Force, Valmont, E. Force, Lawrence, Petro, Johnson, Bugash, Bamat, Warner, Forest.

The Baseball Field at the Grange Fair Grounds in Centre Hall

Wally Moses in 1937

1930's—Nine small Centre County high schools had baseball for many years, while the larger schools (Bellefonte, State College, and Philipsburg) did not.

1937—On August 23, Bellefonte American Legion Post 33 and the Bellefonte Centre County League Team co-sponsored a baseball game between Connie Mack's Philadelphia Athletics of the American League vs. an All-Star team from the County League. The purpose was to dedicate the new Bellefonte Community Baseball Field (presently the BHS Athletic Field).

All-Stars: 3B—Paul Martz*, Jim Gates; SS—Don Lane, Ken Truhn; LF—Gib Anderson*, Bruce Knarr*; CF—Mose Johnston, Gerald Gates; 2B—Al Pletcher, Jack Markle; 1B—Bill Boling; RF—Ran Keller, Bill Bishop; C—Muddy Lucas, Jay Robinson (father of Don Robinson), Carl Gettig. Pitchers and innings pitched: Caleb Roher 4, Curtis Watts 2, Glenn Aumiller* 1, Lefty Whitehill* 1, Joe Confer 1.

The Athletics, coached by Earl Mack (Connie's son), brought the starting team including Chubby Dean and Wally Moses plus five subs; and banged out 11 hits.

The All-Star's Jay Robinson had a single and an RBI, as did Gerald "Peany" Gates; and Glenn Aumiller shut down the pros in his one inning pitched. Aumiller also had a 3-run double; and Bruce Knarr had a triple and scored in the 9th inning.

Portable seating came from Penn State; and 3000 fans paid a $1 admission fee.

A wooden fence surrounded the baseball field; and balls were flying off the A's bats over the fence for a 10-0 lead after 6 innings. "Red" Brown was the president of the Centre County Baseball League at the time which included Bellefonte, State College, Port Matilda, and Beech Creek.

The coaches were Ben Nicodemus, Port Matilda; and Creighton Wheeland, Bellefonte. Umpires were Bill Kline, Bellefonte; and Coaly Hancock, Port Matilda. The batboy was Donald Rechert.

In the 9th inning, there were so many balls hit foul that the home team ran out of baseballs, even though the Athletics had chipped in three. So the game ended with nobody out in the 9th inning and Philadelphia ahead, 10-7.

1941—Bellefonte High School restored baseball to its sports program. Glenn Aumiller, who had previously coached East Penns Valley High School in Millheim, was named coach.

On April 15, Bellefonte was defeated 17-2 by the Reedsville High School Brownies.

1941--The Centre Hall Tigers beat the Red Raiders 3-1. Bellefonte's Woody Johnson was 2 for 4, including a double. Johnny Drogan had an RBI single. Pitcher Lloyd Reese allowed 5 hits and struck out 6. Other Bellefonte players included Johnny Rose, Jim Masullo (Pat Masullo's father), Dick Torsell, and Frank Sciabica.

A game between Bellefonte and State College High Schools was played on May 7 in State College, a 6-5 triumph for the Little Lions. Jim Masullo had a pair of doubles. Gene Barto got the win and Lloyd Reese took the loss.

1942—Coach Aumiller was replaced by Forest Benford, who had previously coached Pleasant Gap High School prior to that school being absorbed into the Bellefonte District. "Benny" played for Pleasant Gap in the County League.

1946—On April 12, Bellefonte High School erupted for 20 runs against Howard, climaxed by center fielder Jim Sellers' grand slam home run in the last inning. Sellers' blow was estimated to be a drive of 400 feet to deep center. Raider sophomore Boyd Thomas collected the win on the hill, and Howard was limited to 2 runs. Fred "Crabby" Gordon and Shawley also smacked three hits in the lopsided victory.

At Philipsburg, Bellefonte topped the Mounties 10-5 on April 30. Jim Sellers had four hits, including two home runs and Joe DeHass had two hits. The winning pitcher was Sellers. Jim Polka took the loss for Philipsburg.

Action at Bellefonte Community Field

1948—Another lopsided victory took place on April 23 as Bellefonte downed Cooper Township 13-4. Right hander Harp McMullen went the distance for the Raiders, striking out six. Bob Nellis went 3 for 4. John Zeleznick, Steve Kucas, Bud Witherite, Chet Fulton, and Boyd Thomas also contributed to the win.

11

1952 Bellefonte High School 7-3 Baseball Team

First Row, L-R: Fred McMullin, Hassel McMullin, Ernie Lucas, Chuck Casper, Max Robison, Harold Coakley. **Row 2:** Manager Ron Jodon, Ken McMullen, Ward Whitehill, Dave Adams, Drew Rice, Bob Davis. **Row 3:** Coach Forest Benford, Bob Witherite, Robert Yeager, Jim Park, Assistant Coach Ralph Dale. **Row 4:** Tom Saxion, Fred Kelley, Bill Hoover.
Not in picture: Ken Moyer, Jack McMullen.

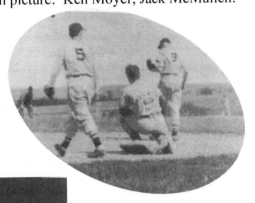

Above: Action at the Bellefonte Community Field.
Left: Ken McMullen.   **Right: Bob Davis**

Wins: Clearfield (9-1 & 5-1); Philipsburg (12-6 & 3-2); Lewistown (9-0 & 5-2); Lock Haven (4-1).
Losses: State College (8-4 & 15-6); LH (4-2).

12

1954 Bellefonte High School Varsity Baseball Team

First Row, L-R: Ron Jodon, Fred Kelley, Gilbert McMurtrie, Jim Funk, Tom Benner, Charlie Gates, Bob MacMillan, Jack McMullen. **Row 2:** Dick Tressler, Harold Shuey, Robert Witherite, Joel Kling, Tom Shultz, Bill Hoover, Hass McMullin, Dick Pierce. **Row 3:** Marvin Breon, Walt Fetzer, Bill Sharp, Emory White, Coach Forest Benford. Absent from photo: Murray Davidson, Clifford Yorks, and Fred Murray.

The Red Raiders ended the season at 6-4. Victories were: Clearfield (18-1 & 5-3), Lock Haven (5-1), State College (13-2), and Philipsburg (6-5 & 4-1). Losses came at the hands of: Lock Haven (8-0), State College (1-0), and Lewistown (2-1 & 6-5).

Tom Benner
Outfield

Jim Funk
Pitcher

Fred Kelley
First Base

Murray Davidson
Third Base

Jack McMullen—2B **Bob MacMillan--OF** **Fred Murray--OF** **Gilbert McMurtrie--SS**

Charlie Gates **Clifford Yorks** **Ronnie Jodon**
Catcher **Pitcher** **Manager**

1955—At Bellefonte on May 3, the Raiders beat Lewistown 7-3. Tom Shultz got the victory while Hass McMullin's two-run single was the difference maker in the first inning for the home team. Right fielder Breon also homered for Bellefonte.

1956—Bellefonte 1, State College 0. Jack Teaman had two hits and Emory White doubled for the Raiders on May 8. The winning pitcher, Bill Sharp, allowed only one hit and struck out 14. Gary Williams, the losing pitcher, allowed 7 hits and struck out 3 for the Little Lions.

1956—On May 17, Miles Township beat Walker Township, 1-0. This Centre County High School Championship game was the last game ever played by either school. Miles Twp. merged with Gregg Twp. Vocational H.S., Centre Hall-Potter High, and East Penns Valley High to form the Penns Valley H.S. in Sept. of 1956. The Walker Township Cardinals became part of Bellefonte High School that fall.

1957 Bellefonte High School 5-4 Baseball Team

First Row, L-R: Earl Yarnell, Emory White, Gerald Styers, Bill Sharp, Jack Witmer, Ken Anderson, Don Shuey, Coach Forest Benford. **Row 2:** Bill Schwartz , Andy Thal, Dick Tressler, Jerry Emerick, Ken Barner, Gerald Corman, Dave Hill, Wayne Long. **Row 3:** Dick Pearce, Robert Taylor, Earl Gettig, Bill Beck, John Stover, Bill Smith, Bill Gummo, Richard Stover. **Row 4:** Assistant Coach Ralph Dale, Ken Eminhizer, Bill Cox, Barry Hayes.

The 10-game schedule included Lewistown; but that game was not played. Wins: Penns Valley (3-2 & 4-0); State College (2-0); Philipsburg (3-2); and Bald Eagle (8-5). Losses: Bald Eagle (6-4); Clearfield (6-5); Philipsburg (10-3); and State College (16-3).

Seniors

L-R: Bill Sharp, Jerry Styers, Wayne Long, Jack Witmer, and Emory White.

1957—First year for the Central Penn Scholastic Baseball League, which consisted of five teams: Bellefonte, Penns Valley, Bald Eagle, Philipsburg, and State College.

Bellefonte Little League
1958 PENNSYLVANIA STATE CHAMPIONS

Front Row, L. - R: Ronald Howard, William Foresman, Thomas Grieb, Dennis Lose, Charles Fletmake Jr., Barry Burger, Larry Kellogg, Danny Kahle.

Second Row: Thomas Crater, Larry Conaway, Dennis Leathers, Michael Ranio Jr., John Sodergren, Rodney Mitchell.

Back Row: Russell Haupt, Coach., Bob Gingerich, Host., Harold Rossman, Manager Frank Webster, Pres., Joseph S. Pisoni, Dist. 10 Director., John M. Lindemuth, Commissioner.

In the semi-final game of the Pennsylvania State Tournament, Rod Mitchell was the hero for Bellefonte in a 5-2, seven inning win over Mill Creek-Seneca. His two-run double in the fifth broke a scoreless tie, and after Mill Creek-Seneca forced extra innings by scoring two in the bottom of the sixth, Mitchell's three-run homer again broke the tie. Winning pitcher Gary Kellogg struck out 13.

In the championship game, Bellefonte rallied for a pair of runs in the bottom of the sixth inning to edge Jessup Carbino. Jessup pitcher Hank Zeino took a perfect game into the sixth, and teammate Bob Cicci's homer had given Jessup a 1-0 lead. However, in the sixth, Bill Foresman and Charlie Fletemake drew walks, and pinch hitter John Sodergren doubled down the right field line to tie the game. One out later, Rod Mitchell lofted a sacrifice fly to right field that plated Sodergren with the winning run.

Most of these youngsters continued with baseball and formed the nucleus of the 1963 Bellefonte High School Baseball Team.

Howard, Lose, Burger, and Conaway returned for the 1964 season.

1958 Bellefonte High School Varsity Baseball Team

First Row, L-R: Dick Leathers, Earl Yarnell, Les McClellan, Ken Anderson, Jerry Emerick, Don Shuey. **Row 2:** Dick Pierce, Walt Krauss, Jack Weber, Gerald Corman, Earl Gettig, Coach Forest Benford. **Row 3:** Nevin Wilkins, Richard Deitrich, Ernest Ebeling, Jim Wilson, Joe Kresovich. **Row 4:** Manager Barry Hayes, Skip Whitehill, Paul King.

The Red Raiders finished with a record of 3-5 in the Central Penn League, and 4-5 overall. Wins: Bald Eagle (7-6 & 5-3); Penns Valley (6-2); and Clearfield (13-7). Losses: State College (8-5 & 10-2); Philipsburg (8-0 & 6-2); and Penns Valley (6-3).

Senior Lettermen, Left to Right:
Earl Yarnell, Ken Anderson, Dick Leathers, Jerry Emerick, Les McClellan.

17

1959 Bellefonte High School Baseball Team

First Row, L-R: Coach Forest L. Benford, Gary Miller, Gerald Corman, Dick Pierce, Don Shuey, Earl Gettig, Jack Weber, Assistant Coach Ralph Dale. **Row 2:** Richard Deitrich, Fred McClellan, Walter Krauss, Bob Bathgate, John McMullin, Joe Kresovich, Harry Whitehill. **Row 3:** Ernest Ebeling, Ellery Seitz, Charles Larimer, Cecil Milton, Douglas Shuey, Kent Wyndham, Jim Wilson.

Dick Pierce   **Don Shuey**   **Earl Gettig**

1959—On April 22, Bellefonte beat Bald Eagle Area, 1-0. An unearned run in the bottom of the Bellefonte first inning was all pitcher Dick Deitrich needed as the Red Raiders won a hard-fought game. Earl Gettig drew a one-out first inning walk and scored on a base hit by Skip Whitehill, aided by a throwing error by the Eagles. Jim Wilson, Ernie Ebeling, and Joe Kresovich had base hits, and Whitehill also tripled in the late innings but was left stranded.

1961—Bellefonte topped Bald Eagle Area, 5-2. Joe Kresovich threw a 5-inning no-hitter in the season's opener on April 17. Home runs by Gary Miller and Jim Hartle in the bottom of the 5th inning were not counted as the rains came, and Umpire Bill Luther called the game. Kresovich fanned 8, and Rod Mitchell along with Skip Whitehill each collected two hits in the abbreviated contest.

1961 Pennsylvania State Babe Ruth League Champions

Bellefonte boys, ages 13-15, were honored by the Governor of Pennsylvania, David L. Lawrence, in his office in Harrisburg.

Kneeling, L-R: Walter Krauss, John Sodergren*, Denny Leathers*, Manager Dick Leathers.
Standing, L-R: Mrs. Conaway, Norm Crater, Dave Eckenrode**, Coach Marlin Conaway, Larry Conaway*, Tom Crater*, Bud Cable, Gary Kellogg*, Barry Burger*, League President Bob Holston, Charlie Doland*, Bill Foresman*, State Representative Bill Moerschbacher, Governor Lawrence, State Senator Jo Hays, Dave Long*, League Treasurer Jack Burger, Ron Howard*, Denny Lose*. Rod Mitchell* is hidden behind Larry Conaway. Absent from photo: Mike Ranio*, Paul Antolosky*, Tom Grieb*.   ***Player**   ****Alternate**

1963 Bellefonte High School Baseball Team

First Row, L-R: George Jodon, Rod Mitchell, Denny McMullin, John Sodergren, Gary Kellogg, Denny Leathers. **Row 2:** Ron Smith, Larry Conaway, Denny Lose, Ron Howard, Charlie Doland, Tom Crater, Grant Lee. **Row 3:** Coach Forest Benford, Bob Breon, Tom Bathgate, Gary Haupt, Louie Johnson, Bob Cathcart. Not in photo: Duane Maloy, Tim Holston, Terry Perryman, Bill Wilkins, Dave Whitehill, Mgrs. John Gentzel and Charlie Fletemake.

The 1963 Red Raiders compiled a Central Penn League record of 5-3; and lost to State College in a league playoff game. Wins: Bald Eagle Area (9-0 & 13-3); Penns Valley (11-7); State College (4-2); and Philipsburg (9-2). Losses: Penns Valley (10-5); State College (2-1); and Philipsburg (4-0).

Shorty Stoner out-dueled Denny Leathers in a league playoff game, as the Little Lions edged the Red Raiders, 2-1, ending Bellefonte's season with a 5-4 record.

At right: Forest Benford, Head Coach.

At right: Ralph Dale, Assistant Coach.

Seniors, L-R: Denny McMullin, John Sodergren, Denny Leathers, Rod Mitchell, George Jodon.

Ralph Dale played for Boalsburg in the Centre County Baseball League in 1929. He led the 36-12 club with 37 hits and 21 runs scored.

1963 Bellefonte Bench Photos

1963—Pitcher Denny Leathers allowed 2 hits and struck out 11, as the Raiders beat State College 4-2 on April 26. Shorty Stoner took the loss for the Little Lions who allowed 10 hits and struck out 5. Dave Long, Larry Conaway, and Charlie Doland each collected two hits for Bellefonte, whose lineup included John Sodergren, Gary Kellogg, Rod Mitchell, Ron Howard and Denny McMullin.

1963—On May 2, Gary Kellogg, Ron Howard, and Charlie Doland had 2 hits apiece as Bellefonte routed rival Bald Eagle Area 13-3. Rod Mitchell, John Sodergren, and Larry Conaway also contributed to the victory which put the Red Raiders atop the Central Penn League at 4-0.

1964—Don Robinson replaced Forest Benford as head coach of the Bellefonte High School baseball team. Ralph Gray was hired as assistant coach, replacing Ralph Dale.

1964

**Left:
Head Coach
Don Robinson.**

**Right:
Assistant
Coach
Ralph
Gray.**

Donald Harpster Robinson

1948

Don "Robby" Robinson was born on July 28, 1940, in Philipsburg, Pa.,with a baseball pedigree. His father, Jay Robinson, played a year as a minor league catcher in the St. Louis Cardinal organization, and continued to play ball with Port Matilda in the Centre County League. Jay was a player-manager in 1948 when his son Don was the batboy for the "Porters" who won the league championship.

1958

His uncle, Merrill Harpster, played for the Porters in 1939; and a nephew of his mother; "Peany" Gates, played for Penn State.

Robby began playing little league in Port Matilda as a 6-year old; and in 1951, he and his brother Jay hitch-hiked to Unionville to play junior league ball. Robby also played junior league in Tyrone.

He earned two letters in baseball for Port Matilda High in 1955-56, and two letters in 1957 -1958 as a second baseman playing for Coach "Doc" Etters in the newly-formed Bald Eagle Area District.

1962

Fulfilling a life-long dream, Robinson suited up for the Penn State Varsity for three years, winning a letter as a starter at third base in 1961 and at second base in 1962. Coach Joe Bedenk batted Robby second in the lineup due to his ability to get on base and sacrifice bunt. He played errorless baseball for the Nittany Lions.

The road trips, the friendships developed, and the discipline Bedenk created remained in his memory. He also learned on the road trips that "dippy eggs" were not on the breakfast menu.

1974

Robinson graduated from Penn State in 1962; and was hired at Bellefonte, where he taught Junior High Phys. Ed. and Science, and coached basketball. He became the head baseball coach at Bellefonte High School in 1964, and the Raiders promptly won the league championship. In his 18 years as head coach, his Red Raiders won seven Central Penn League Titles and four District VI Championships. Robby learned a lot from Bedenk, who stressed pitching, defense, moving the runners, and fundamentals. However, by his own admission, he learned the most baseball at Bellefonte High School

After taking a sabbatical in 1982, he returned to coaching baseball at Bellefonte as an assistant to Denny Leathers for another 18 years.

1990

From 1956-88, his love of baseball and strong desire to win kept him playing in the Centre County League with teams that included Unionville, Port Matilda, State College, Centre Hall, and Bellefonte.

Robinson and his wife Linda live in Bellefonte and have one son, Jon, daughters Julie and Jodie, and four grandchildren.

Robby at Penn State

Don Robinson enrolled at Penn State in 1958 with the hope of getting a degree in Physical Education and playing baseball for the Nittany Lions.

Robinson

In the spring of 1959, he played on the Penn State freshman team for Coach Bill Spieth and beat out 6 candidates at 2nd base, including Buck Riden from Kishacoquillas, who eventually became the head baseball coach at Indian Valley.

Robby would often jog up to watch the varsity practice after his workout with the freshman team was finished; and one day Coach Joe Bedenk asked him to go out and help Larry Fegley[1], a great hitter, with his pivot at second base. Bedenk had seen Robby play in the County Baseball League, an organization of which the Lion mentor was not a big fan.

In the 1960 season, Coach Bedenk saw in sophomore Don Robinson the kind of baseball player he wanted—not blessed with size, speed, or strength, but having the enthusiasm which shows when a player runs on and off the field instead of walking.

Bedenk was concerned about his team's lack of hitting and sloppy fielding; so Robby's ability to get the bat on the ball and his errorless fielding landed him a position on the varsity[2].

The Lions fell to Colgate, 4-3, on April 20 in a 12-inning contest; but Robinson had a 2-out single in the 9th inning.

On April 23, in a double-header against Georgetown in Washington, D.C., Robby replaced Captain Dick Landis at third base. Landis was in a slump and Robinson had looked good hitting and had no miscues in the field.

In the West Virginia game on April 27, Robby led off instead of batting second.

Robinson's 2-out double in the Lafayette game on April 29 drove in the winning run in a 3-2 Penn State victory.

On May 4, in a 7-0 win over Bucknell, Robby had a sacrifice and 2 singles— each hit producing a run-batted-in.

The switch to third base from his normal second base spot took its toll on Robby's arm and required a different kind of focus—balls got there quicker and one had to be aware of how hard the ball was hit and where the play was going to be. In practice one day Ed Kikla, a left-handed batter, lined a ball that hit below Robby's left eye and broke his infra-orbital plate. That didn't deter him from going to practice the next day, but he became more alert at the "hot corner".

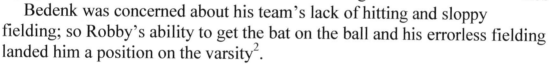

---

[1] In the 1960 season, Fegley was named to the NCAA All-American Team and was a District II All-Star.
[2] Don Robinson is the only Bald Eagle Area athlete to play three years of varsity baseball at Penn State.

THE PENNSYLVANIA STATE UNIVERSITY
University Park, Pennsylvania

1960 BASEBALL SCHEDULE

				NAME	NO
Apr.	6	Gettysburg	University Park, Penna.	Rentzel	1
	9	Syracuse (DH)	University Park, Penna.	Robinson	2
	13	Villanova	Villanova, Penna.	Landis	3
	14	Pennsylvania	Philadelphia, Penna.	Benton	4
	16	Ithaca	University Park, Penna.	Suplizo	5
	20	Colgate (DH)	University Park, Penna.	Hrobak	6
	23	Georgetown (DH)	Washington, D. C.	Fegley	7
	27	West Virginia	University Park, Penna.	DeLong	8
	29	Lafayette	Easton, Penna.	Beans	9
	30	Rutgers	New Brunswick, N. J.	McGraw	10
May	4	Bucknell	University Park, Penna.	Davis	11
	7	Maryland	University Park, Penna.	Bruni	12
	10	Bucknell	Lewisburg, Penna.	Durbin	14
	11	Lehigh	Bethlehem, Penna.	Decaspers	15
	14	Navy	University Park, Penna.	Kikla	16
	18	Temple	University Park, Penna.	Phillips	17
	21	Pittsburgh (DH)	Pittsburgh, Penna.	Adams	18
	26	Delaware	Newark, Del.	Arner	19

COACH: F. J. Bedenk   CAPTAIN: Richard Landis

MANAGER: Gilbert Kahn

NAME	NO
Bergey	20
Kochman	21
Biesecker	22
Beighey	23
Freedman	
Chapala	
McSparran	
Burkhardt	
Whorral	
Campbell	
Riden	

Robby was always sharply dressed for a game, and he used to tell his players at Bellefonte High that it didn't require much talent to look good in a uniform.

The 1960 team finished the season with a 9-9 record. Bedenk was assisted by Chuck "Stud" Medlar, who pitched the first round of batting practice each day. Roger Kochman once hit a line drive that caught Medlar on the left thigh; but the huge guy continued to pitch and ended up with a bruise that looked as big as a basketball.

Medlar coached pitchers and catchers and hit outfield.

Roger Kochman, #21, an outfielder, also played football for the Nittany Lions. He once missed the baseball bus for an away game; but a friend drove him to Potter's Mills, where he caught up with his teammates.

In March of the 1961 season, the Penn State Baseball Team had a 5-day stay in Fort Eustis, Virginia, for pre-season drills. Coach Bedenk planned to use Robby at second base and have him bat against right-handed pitchers.

However, Bedenk went with Bart Brodkin at second and Robinson returned to third base as a starter and hit second in the lineup due to his ability to bunt and get on base.

Robinson

On April 5, in the season's opener against Gettysburg, Robby had two hits, and drove in the winning run with a 2-run double in a 3-2 victory over the Bullets.

In a 5-3 win against Maryland on April 24, he batted second and continued his flawless play in the field.

Robby injured his shoulder in the Navy game, which nagged him the rest of his baseball career. The injury kept him from signing with the N.Y. Mets his senior year.

The 1961 Baseball Schedule, Results, and Roster

April 5	Penn State 3	Gettysburg 2	Jonas
8	Penn State 6	Villanova 9	Brodkin
22	Penn State 3	Lafayette 2	Rodenhaver
24	Penn State 5	Maryland 3	Robinson
May 3	Penn State 15	Rutgers 2	Capt. DeLong
9	Penn State 3	Navy 4	Adams
12	Penn State 0	Colgate 7	Pae
13	Penn State 0	Syracuse 10	Thomas
13	Penn State 2	Syracuse 3	DeCaspers
18	Penn State 7	Bucknell 0	Fenton
20	Penn State 14	Pittsburgh 1	Bergey
20	Penn State 6	Pittsburgh 2	Gieguez
23	Penn State 4	Temple 1	Biesecker
25	Penn State 6	Delaware 4	Hrobak
25	Penn State 1	Delaware 2	Durbin

The team finished with a 9-6 record. Football players on the 1961 baseball team: Galen Hall, Don Jonas, Bill Saul, Dick Pae, Al Gursky. Don Robinson earned his first varsity letter at Penn State in 1961.

Kikla
Manager Engle
Husk
Capt. Elect Phillips
Gursky
Saul
Shaffer

Assistant Coach Chuck Medlar was a native of Johnstown. He taught a training course at Penn State and was the trainer for the football and baseball teams.

1962 Penn State Varsity Baseball Team
First Row, L-R: Gursky, Light, Felton, Pae, Werner, Jonas, Brodkin, Bee, Robinson, DeCaspers, Liske. Row 2: Coach Bedenk, Fenton, Bergey, Stallman, Spanier, Noe, Biesecker, Phillips, Gieguez, Paris, Kochman, Captain-Elect Anderson, Assistant Coach Medlar.

THE PENNSYLVANIA STATE UNIVERSITY
University Park, Pennsylvania

1962 BASEBALL SCHEDULE

April	3	Gettysburg	W	University Park, Pa.
	6	Lehigh	W	Bethlehem, Pa.
	7	Villanova	—	Villanova, Pa.
	10	Ithaca	W - 14 - 5	University Park, Pa.
	13	Rutgers	—	New Brunswick, N. J.
	14	Army	W - 8 - 3	West Point, N. Y.
	17	Pennsylvania		Philadelphia, Pa.
	24	Bucknell		University Park, Pa.
May	1	Maryland		University Park, Pa.
	2	Lafayette		Easton, Pa.
	5	Navy		University Park, Pa.
	8	Colgate		University Park, Pa.
	12	Syracuse (DH)		University Park, Pa.
	15	West Virginia		University Park, Pa.
	17	Bucknell		Lewisburg, Pa.
	19	Pittsburgh (DH)		Pittsburgh, Pa.
	22	Temple		University Park, Pa.
	24	Delaware		Newark, Del.

COACH: F. J. Bedenk   CAPTAIN: John Phillips

MANAGER: Fred Engle

The 1962 team had a record of 10-3 in the regular season, but lost to Ithaca, 7-6 on June 1 in a NCAA District II Playoff.

Ace pitcher Bob Fenton, a junior, won 8 games in the 1962 season.

In a double-header with Syracuse, pitcher Dave Giusti of Pittsburgh Pirate fame, threw a shutout against the Lions, and played center field in the second game, a 3-2 win for the Orangemen.

Football players: Dick Pae, Pete Liske, Roger Kochman, Dick Anderson, Don Jonas, Al Gursky.

PENN STATE ROSTER	
NAME	NO.
Hock	1
Robinson	2
Decaspers	3
Pae	4
Liske	5
Light	6
Brodkin	7
Mance	8
Stellman	9
Spanier	10
Fenton	11
Bergey	12
Mosier	14
Paris	15
Werner	16
Schrecker	17
Kochman	18
Noe	19
Phillips	20
Kozusko	21
Biesecker	22
Dobrosielski	23
Bee	26
Felton	28
Carnwath	29
Anderson	30
Wert	32
Jonas	33
Zaccagni	34
Gursky	35

In the 1962 season, Robinson moved from third base to second. He won the starting job in a battle with Bart Brodkin (the regular second baseman in 1961) and Dick Mance.

According to Coach Bedenk, Robby was one of the slowest men in the starting lineup despite that Robby stole 4 bases in the opening game with Gettysburg on April 3, and his steal in the third inning was a big play. Bedenk stated that Robinson typically got a good jump on the pitcher.

Don Robinson dives into first base safely after being picked off and getting in a rundown in the Maryland game.

Roger Kochman (18) and Don Robinson greet teammate Fred Light after he hit a home run against Bucknell.

Coach Robinson always reminded his players at Bellefonte High, "If you're dumb enough to get picked off, you'd better be smart enough to get out of it."

Batting in the second spot in the lineup, Robinson walked, scored, and had a hit in an 8-4 victory over Army on April 14.

According to Bedenk, second baseman Don Robinson and shortstop John Phillips were two of the most consistent Lions in reaching base.

After routing Bucknell 25-6 with Bob Fenton on the mound, Robby raised his average from .263 to .308 with a three for seven performance. Only Captain Phillips had a higher average.

Phillips also played basketball for the Lions. Fenton was a Philipsburg product.

**Don Robinson   John Phillips
KEYSTONE COMBINATION**

Don Robinson hustles to first base and beats the throw from Temple second baseman Rick Simon, who bobbled the ball. Robinson reached base four times as the Lions beat the Owls, 4-2.

Don Robinson (2) takes third baseman Fred Light's throw to double up Syracuse's Dick Taylor. The Lions won both ends of a twin bill, 4-0 and 7-6.

Bellefonte High School Coach Don Robinson always told his players, "It doesn't take any talent to hustle on the ball field."

Robby had a perfect fielding average in the 1962 season while winning his second varsity letter.

L-R: **Shortstop John Phillips, third baseman Fred Light, second baseman Don Robinson, and first baseman Pete Liske** have their eyes set on an important doubleheader with Pitt.

Bedenk was a disciplinarian; and his Lions wore a coat and tie on road trips.

PENN STATE (10-3)

Probable Starters

No. White-Gray		Player
4	4	Dick Pae, CF (.259)
2	2	Don Robinson, 2B (.222)
6	6	Fred Light, 3B (.298)
20	20	John Phillips, SS (.432)
30	24	Dick Anderson, RF (.269)
33	33	Don Jonas, C (.286)
18	18	Roger Kochman, LF (.293)
5	5	Pete Liske, 1B (.158)

Reserves and Pitchers

7	7	Bart Brodkin, IF (.000)
9	9	Dick Stellman, P (0-0)
10	10	Jeff Spanier, P (0-1)
11	11	Bob Fenton, P (8-1)
12	12	Dave Bergey, P (0-1)
14	14	Chet Mosier, P (0-0)
16	16	Grier Werner, IF (.000)
19	19	Dick Noe, P (0-0)
22	22	Marlin Biesecker, P (2-0)
26	21	Dick Bee, C (.000)
28	30	Jim Felton, P (0-0)
35	23	Al Gursky, OF (.000)

Coach: Joe Bedenk
Captain: John Phillips

Robby in the County League

What does a man who loves baseball do in the summer months? He looks for an opportunity to be on a team and play the game.

Robby's father, Jay Robinson, who played a year of minor league ball in the St. Louis Cardinal organization, was the catcher on the Port Matilda "Porters," made up largely of men who worked in the McFeely Brickyard in town. As a youngster, Robby dreamed of the day when he could join his dad on the team; and the opportunity came when he was 14 years old on a day when the Porters didn't have enough men to fill the lineup.

Jay made a white "X" between first and second base so his son would know where to play. Although he wasn't a regular, Robby continued to practice with the team every evening until he made the starting lineup at second base. His tenure with Port Matilda lasted until 1967.

The Porters were champions of the Centre County Baseball League in 1948. Robby idolized those players, one of whom, Dick Smith, set county records with 88 hits in 217 at-bats for a .406 average and 76 runs scored. Smith was a Port Matilda High School graduate, and in 1948 played for both the Porters and the Bellefonte VFW teams. Smith soon signed with the Pittsburgh Pirates and had a good professional career before retiring.

In 1951 Port Matilda won the Western Division of the Centre County League; but lost in the finals to Centre Hall.

Don Robinson pitched for Port in 1961, and won 5-4 over Clarence. He had 3 of Port's 4 hits; and led the league in hits (24) and doubles (6) for the season.

Robinson joined a Clarence team in 1960 that had previously made three straight appearances in the National Baseball Congress Baseball Tournament in Midland, Pennsylvania. That year, the "Hilltoppers" won the championship.

In 1965, Robby played on a Tyrone team that won the Altoona Greater City League Title.

Just playing baseball didn't satisfy Robby; he wanted to win. In 1967, he was contacted by Dean Witherite, who wanted him to join the State College County League Team. He accepted, and the talent-laden squad won four straight championships in his four years with the Collegians.

In 1968, in the best-of-five finals between State College and Millheim, Robby had a single in Game 1 and 3 hits in Game 4 including a home run, which gave his team the championship in an 11-3 victory.

In State College's second championship, Robinson's batting average was .317 with no errors in 156 chances and led the league in hits (39) and runs scored (36).

Robby as a "Porter"

Don Robinson continued to participate in the Centre County League where the best brand of baseball was being played. Baseball was a sport where he could be successful and improve the quality of his play and of course—win.

Centre Hall received his services in 1971, where he teamed up with Denny Leathers. Robby hit a home run in a series with Clarence and drove in 3 runs. His hit total for the season was 38.

Playing for Bellefonte in a 1980 game against State College, Robby, Greg Brown, and Denny Leathers hit home runs in the same inning. In the County Tournament, Robinson homered against Howard, eliminating the Hawks.

Also in 1980, Robby played for Bellefonte in the Howard Baseball Tournament.

Playing for Bellefonte against Centre Hall in 1984, the Governors were down 9-8 in the last inning when Robinson hit a home run to tie the game; and two walks later, teammate Randy McMullen hit a 3-run homer to win the game.

Bellefonte won the league championship in 1982 and 1984 with Robinson.

In 1985 the Bellefonte Governors[3] defeated Howard in the semi-finals, 6-5, on Robby's home run in the bottom of the 8th inning. Wayne Haas's first pitch went sailing over the fence, giving Bellefonte pitcher Dave Klinefelter the win.

1988 was the final baseball season in the Centre County League for Don Robinson. He was 48 years old at the time; but teammate Ward Whitehill was still pitching at age 53.

Don Robinson, in his 34 years in the County League, got to play with or against guys he competed with, coached with, or coached at Bellefonte High School in his 36 years as the head coach and assistant to Denny Leathers.

In 1948, Dick Smith of Port Matilda had a try-out with the Pirates at the Port ball field. Eight-year old Don Robinson, who was excused from class that afternoon, was thrilled to help retrieve balls that were hit to the outfield. The Pirates signed Smith, assigned him to a minor league team, and he played parts of 5 seasons (1951-55) with Pittsburgh. During Robby's senior season at Penn State in 1962, Dick Smith was an assistant coach for the Lions and an instructor in the Penn State Phys. Ed. Department. Robinson and Smith would sit together on the bus to away games and talk baseball.

---

[3]Seven men who have been elected governor once called Bellefonte home. William Bigler (1813-1880), William F. Packer (1807-1870), Andrew Gregg Curtin (1816-1894), James A. Beaver (1837-1914), and Daniel H. Hastings (1849-1903) were governors of Pennsylvania. John Bigler (1805-1856) was governor of California, and Robert J. Walker (1801-1869) was a territorial governor of Kansas.

Robby—A Winning Baseball Coach

The biggest influence on Don Robinson's life and his coaching was his father, Jay Robinson, an outstanding athlete in his day. Jay's knowledge of the game and his skill as a baseball player were impressive. Once in a County League game he was pitching right-handed and halfway through the contest he suddenly became a southpaw.

Jay Robinson would hit ground balls to Robby and his older brother Jay in the backyard of their Port Matilda home and made it competitive. One boy would be Bucknell and the other would be Penn State. The elder Robinson was most likely influenced by the coaching prowess of one Carl G. Snavely, who coached football and baseball at the Bellefonte Academy and won national acclaim; and later became the head coach of football and baseball at Bucknell University.

Jay Robinson in 1939
Catcher, Port Matilda Porters

Robby was never pushed into baseball by his dad; but he encouraged him to use the talents he possessed.

Being in close proximity to the town of Philipsburg, Robby's father would watch the Mounties' games and the pair would sit down and talk baseball for hours at a time.

The 1951 Port Matilda-McFeely Brickyard Baseball Team was a major influence on Don Robinson. As an 11-year old, he would attend the team practices; and the guys would let him to play second base during batting practice.

He idolized those ballplayers and couldn't wait to be one of the town team players.
First Row, L-R: John Woodring, Penny Weller, Lester Daughenbaugh. **Row 2:** Gilbert Woodring, Earl Dorman, Gerry Woodring, George Rhule. **Row 3:** Roy Stimer, Umpire Larry Ross, Chester Stimer, Sam Stiver

Weller gave the little guy his first and *last* chew of tobacco. After that experience, Robby switched to bubble gum.

31

Coach Don Robinson knew the rules of baseball; and when a call went against his team, he didn't hesitate to go out and argue his point with the umpire.

In the photo at the left, Robby and Umpire Charlie Breon discuss the rule of what constitutes a check swing as Bellefonte batter Bruce Baney listens.

Charlie Breon quite often was one of the umpires when the Red Raiders played at State College. In the photo below, Robby shows his displeasure with a Breon call that went against his team.

One of the best umpires in the Central Penn League was Jake Salsgiver, who was a former player in the Centre County Baseball League.

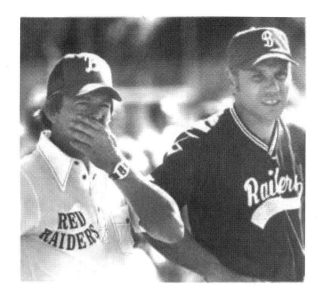 

Don Robinson and Ralph Gray   **Denny Leathers and Don Robinson**

Robinson praised his assistant coaches—Ralph Gray who handled the junior varsity squad and Denny Leathers, who worked with the pitchers. He had appreciation for their efforts in stressing fundamentals, demanding a total commitment to the sport and adding to the abilities that their players inherited.

According to Don Robinson, the most important factor in the development of baseball talent in Bellefonte was the opportunity for a youngster to play the game. The Little League stressed fundamentals at an age when a boy or girl was receptive to learning. The ballplayers continued through the system to Teener League where they mastered the skills which were necessary to win baseball games. The town of Bellefonte supported baseball, as evidenced by the large annual turnout of boys for the junior varsity and varsity baseball programs.

Robby was able to get the most out of his players. He knew what to say to a player at the right time. He had a cunning mind for coaching baseball and his relaxed manner helped the ball club a great deal. He made practice and games enjoyable with his knack for cracking jokes and telling stories.

There was a lot of focus on details during a Robinson practice, which involved hard work and much time spent on execution and sound preparation—as well as many hours spent on fundamentals.

Robby wanted his players to enjoy practice and reminded them that the first three letters of the word "fundamentals" were F-U-N. He told the boys after many practices that, "Practice doesn't make you perfect— 'perfect practice' makes you perfect. You will play the game the way your practice."

A Bellefonte baseball club coached by Don Robinson rarely beat itself, due to few mistakes. The opponents usually beat themselves. The Raiders worked on game situations a lot in practice along with theories of the game.

Winning baseball teams became a tradition at Bellefonte High School when Robby took over the program in 1964.

1964 Bellefonte High School Baseball Team

First Row, L-R: Coach Don Robinson, Assistant Coach Ralph Gray, Denny Lose, Larry Conaway, Grant Lee, Ron Howard, Charlie Doland, Manager Mark Carlson. **Row 2:** Manager Howard Sodergren, Steve McCulley, Joe Menna, Bill Wilkins, Dave Long, Dave Whitehill, Tom Bathgate. **Row 3:** Barry Hinds, Fred Walker, Leroy Smith, Barry Burger, Terry Perryman, Bob Wilkins, Richard Yarnell. **Row 4:** Bob Yarnell, Bob Radick, John Jones, Bill Shuey, Sam McMurtrie, Duane Maloy.

Four lettermen—Ron Howard, Charlie Doland, Dave Long, and Larry Conaway formed the nucleus for the 1964 Bellefonte High School Baseball Team. Those four, along with Denny Lose and Barry Burger, were on the Bellefonte Teener team that won a state championship in 1961.

Key losses from the 1963 Raider squad were: Denny Leathers, John Sodergren, Rod Mitchell, and Gary Kellogg. The entire outfield and most of the pitching were also gone, and Don Robinson, in his first year at the helm of the Tribe, had a young and inexperienced pitching corps.

Robinson was assisted by Ralph Gray.

Other Central Penn League head coaches in the 1964 season were: Bob Smith, State College; John McMullen, Penns Valley; Don Etters, Bald Eagle Area; and Gerry Davis, Philipsburg-Osceola.

The 1964 Red Raiders were the first Bellefonte baseball team to finish the regular season undefeated. The Tribe was 8-0 with victories over: Penns Valley (9-4 & 2-1); State College (4-3 & 8-4); Bald Eagle Area (5-3 & 3-2); and Philipsburg (7-5 & 7-6).

In the District 6 Playoffs, the Raiders tied Hollidaysburg 4-4 in a game called due to darkness; then won the re-scheduled game, 5-1. Lewistown eliminated Bellefonte, 7-5.

The Red Raiders opened the 1964 season at Spring Mills on Wednesday, April 15, with a 9-4 victory. After spotting Penns Valley two runs in the first inning, they took the lead in the 6th when they scored four times on 5 hits and 2 walks. Charlie Doland and Ron Howard were perfect at the plate for Bellefonte, each going 3 for 3. Larry Conaway had 2 hits for the Raiders, and pitcher Terry Perryman scattered 5 hits and struck out 11 for his first win.

Jeff Wert pitched the first five and a third innings and took the loss. He was also called upon to pitch the 7th inning to check a Raider rally. Marty Ilgen hit a solo home run in the 7th for the Rams. Bellefonte had 12 hits and stranded 14. Ilgen played four years of varsity baseball for Penns Valley.

Sophomore Dave Whitehill pitched a 3-hitter against State College at Community Field on Friday, April 17, for his first win; and the 4-3 victory enabled Bellefonte to keep pace with Philipsburg, who was also undefeated.

Dave Long drew a walk to start the game and Larry Conaway singled. Denny Lose attempted to move the runners up with a sacrifice bunt, but the throw to third was late and the bases were full of Indians. Ed Temple retired the next two hitters but Ron Howard hit a shot to second that was misplayed and two runs scored.

Bellefonte added two more runs in the 3rd on singles by Tom Bathgate and Ron Howard, along with two miscues by State College.

Whitehill lost his bid for a no-hitter in the 5th when the Little Lions scored three times. A single, a sacrifice, a balk followed by a walk, two Raider errors and a 2-out double accounted for the runs.

Long, Conaway, and Howard each had two hits for the winners.

The Tribe stranded 10 runners, while State stranded one in each inning.

At right: Scorekeeper/Manager Mark Carlson (left) and Coach Don Robinson (right) along with Bellefonte players mob pitcher Dave Whitehill (#20) after his 4-3 win over State High at Community Field in State College.

On Friday, April 24, the Red Raiders downed Bald Eagle Area, 5-3, at Unionville for their third straight win.

Down 3-1 after one inning, Bellefonte tied the game in the 4th on a single by Tom Bathgate, walks to Duane Maloy and Barry Burger, a Dave Long single and Larry Conaway's fielder's choice.

In the top of the 7th inning, Conaway singled off Terry Dorman, but was thrown out at the plate on a double by Denny Lose. Lose ended up on third on a throwing error by the Eagle catcher and scored the go-ahead run when he stole home with Charlie Doland at bat. Ron Howard singled, stole second, and scored the final Raider run on another Eagle error.

Barry Burger got his first win, giving up 5 hits, 3 runs, and striking out six.

Bellefonte jumped out to a 1-0 lead against Penns Valley in the 2nd inning at the Athletic Field on Monday, May 4, on a one-out walk to Barry Hinds and a double by Tom Bathgate.

The Rams tied the game in the 3rd inning on an error, a stolen base, another error, and a steal of home.

In the bottom of the 3rd, the Raiders scored again on a one-out error, a wild pitch, and Charlie Doland's double. Actually, Doland hit what seemed to be a booming home run, but failed to touch third base.

In the 2-1 Tribe win, Dave Whitehill only gave up 2 hits, struck out 8, and improved his record to 2-0.

His mound opponent, Marlin Bowersox, held the Raiders to 2 hits and struck out 5 in absorbing the loss, which eliminated Penns Valley from title consideration. Bellefonte took over first place in the league with a 4-0 record.

In the 1964 season, Marlin Bowersox with 9 hits was second to Bald Eagle's Barry Ellenberger in batting average in the Central Penn Baseball League at .429. Ellenberger hit .476 with 10 hits.

Bob Luse of Penns Valley was the 1963 batting champion.

In 1964, Bellefonte was led by Larry Conaway with 10 hits for a .357 average in the CPL; Denny Lose had 9 hits for a .310 average; Dave Long hit .304 with 7 hits. Ron Howard also had 7 hits for a .304 average.

Conaway led the league in runs scored—10

On Tuesday, May 5, the Red Raiders eliminated State College from the Central Penn League race with an 8-4 win at the Athletic Field in Bellefonte.

The Little Lions scored twice off starter Barry Burger in the first inning; and State's starter Denny Weaver held the Tribe hitless until the 3rd inning. A walk to Grant Lee, a Burger single, and a sacrifice bunt put runners on second and third. Larry Conaway's sac fly and a single by Denny Lose tied the score at 2. Weaver walked Charlie Doland; and Pete Shutt came in and shut the door on the Raiders.

State College regained the lead in the 4th on a 2-base Bellefonte error and a 2-out single by Gene Rossman; but the Tribe came back in their half of the inning. A double by Barry Hinds, a passed ball, and a suicide squeeze by Lee tied the game at 3.

In the 5th inning, Dave Long singled and scored on Conaway's 2-run homer off Shutt. Singles by Doland and Ron Howard chased Shutt; and reliever Ed Temple's wild pitch scored Doland, putting the Raiders up, 6-3.

Lose's single in the 6th inning drove in two Raiders; and in the top of the 7th, a Burger walk and two Bellefonte bobbles ended the scoring at 8-4.

Burger went the distance, giving up 5 hits and striking out 11 for his second win.

At right: Raider Coach Don Robinson shows his consternation as his Tribe falls behind rival State College early in the game.

Bellefonte's game with Philipsburg at Power Line Field was originally scheduled for April 24; but due to postponements, the game wasn't played until Wed., May 6. At that time the Raiders were 5-0 and in first place in the league; and the Mounties were in second with a 4-0 record. The remaining teams had been eliminated; so the league race was down to Bellefonte and Philipsburg.

Raider mentor Don Robinson decided to go with pitcher Terry Perryman, who went 5 and a third innings, giving up 3 hits, 4 runs, and striking out 7 for his second win. Dave Whitehill was effective in relief, giving up one run on 3 hits in his one and two-thirds innings.

The visitors got on the board in the first inning on singles by Dave Long and Larry Conaway and an infield out by Denny Lose.

Bellefonte added on in the 2nd on a walk to Barry Hinds, an error, a sacrifice, a Long walk, and Conaway's bases-clearing double for a 5-0 lead.

The Mounties scored twice in the bottom half of the 2nd on a 3-base Raider error, a sac fly, a double by Bill Abbott, and another error.

In the 4th inning, a wild pitch and a clutch single by Denny Lose scored a run. A Hinds hit, a walk and a 2-out Perryman hit ended Bellefonte's scoring in the 5th.

The Mounties of Coach Gerry Davis kept battling; and loaded the bases on 3 walks in the 6th. Dave Whitehill relieved Perryman; but Dick Condo's single and a fielder's choice narrowed the gap to 7-4.

In the bottom of the 7th, Philipsburg added another run on 2 singles, a passed ball, and a sac fly by Greg Stine. With the tying runs on base and 2 outs, Charlie Doland made a great play on a ball hit to short as his throw to first beat the runner by half a step, giving Bellefonte a 7-5 victory.

Conaway, Lose, and Perryman each had 2 hits. Ron Howard had a double and played great defense for the Tribe. Sankey gave up 10 hits, 7 runs and had 5 K's.

Philipsburg had two outstanding right-handed pitchers—Bo Sankey and Bill Rech. In the 2nd inning of that game against the Mounties, Bellefonte had runners at second and third with two outs and left-handed hitting Dave Long up to bat. Davis decided to play the percentages and intentionally walked Long to get to Larry "Hoppy" Conaway, a right-handed swinger. Robby walked up to Conaway, a contact hitter, and to make sure he stayed relaxed, told him "I would love to be in your situation. I have a lot of confidence in you. Go up to the plate relaxed and hit your pitch—not the pitcher's pitch." Hoppy responded by getting the clutch hit, and the Raiders won the game. After the game Robby told Hoppy that he had a lot of confidence in his ability as a line-drive hitter; and because he was so focused he wanted him up to bat in a clutch situation.

The Raiders had a close call at the Athletic Field in Bellefonte on Tuesday, May 12, against Bald Eagle Area. Starting pitcher Terry Perryman walked Tony Little and Paul Haas homered; and the Eagles took their 2-0 lead into the 7th inning.

Grant Lee got aboard in the bottom of the 7th with a bunt single. With 2 outs, Dave Long singled and an error put runners on second and third. Larry Conaway walked to load the bases, and Denny Lose poked an opposite-field single to left driving in two, and Conaway also scored on a throwing error for a 3-2 win.

Perryman went five and a third innings, allowing 2 runs on 7 hits and striking out 4. Barry Burger relieved Perryman in the 6th and shut down the Eagles, picking up his third win. Bald Eagle's Chambers gave up 6 hits along with the 3 runs and took the loss. Denny Lose was the only 2-hit man for Bellefonte.

The Raiders celebrate after Denny Lose's game winning single in the seventh inning.

On May 15, Don Robinson's Red Raiders came from behind for the fourth time in the season to win a ball game. Down 5-2 to Philipsburg in the third, Bellefonte cut the lead to 5-3 in its half of the inning when Denny Lose homered to right. Charlie Doland followed with a single, but was erased on a double play.

The Tribe went up 6-5 in the 4th on a double by Barry Hinds, singles by Tom Bathgate and Grant Lee, two stolen bases and two Mountie errors.

Philipsburg tied the game in the 5th inning on a single by Bo Sankey, a stolen base, and two infield outs.

Bellefonte went back on top in the 6th. Grant Lee singled off pitcher Bill Rech's glove, stole second, and took third on Dave Long's infield out. Larry Conaway's grounder was misplayed by the Mounties and Lee scored easily.

In the 7th inning, Mountie speedster John Pedrazzani was on second with one out when Bo Sankey hit a line drive to right fielder Tom Bathgate who caught the ball and fired a strike to Ron Howard at third base to double up Pedrazzani, giving Bellefonte a 7-6 victory and the Central Penn League Title.

Barry Burger pitched well for the Raiders, giving up 6 runs on 6 hits, striking out 5 and allowing only one free pass in picking up his fourth win. Philipsburg's Bill Rech gave up 7 hits along with 7 runs, allowed one walk and struck out four.

At left:

Raider right fielder Tom Bathgate's perfect throw to Ron Howard at third base doubles up Philipsburg speedster John Pedrazzani after he tagged up at second base.

Left to Right: Pitcher Barry Burger, Coach Don Robinson, and Catcher Larry Conaway.

Coach Robinson and Coach Gray received post-game showers in the Bellefonte locker room at the hands of the jubilant Raider players after going 8-0 and winning their first Central Penn League Championship.

Robby's coach at Penn State, Joe Bedenk, watched the game.

1964 Raiders—Hits and Batting Average in Central Penn League:
Charlie Doland—7, .292   Tom Bathgate—6, .250
Grant Lee—4, .174

In his first year at the helm of the Red Raiders in 1964, Robby went up to the senior high faculty room to see Athletic Director "Big John" Miller about getting the field ready for a game at 4 p.m. that day. He didn't really know Big John at that time, who was sitting in his favorite chair in a corner of the "Blue Room," smoking one of his Piedmont cigarettes during his lunch break.

Robby pointed out that the field needed dragged and lined for the game; and Miller asked him who he was getting to get the work done. Robby then asked him, "What are you doing over your lunch hour?"

The other faculty members in the room were in awe and later said that Miller's mouth came open and nothing came out.

Robby was reminded of that incident many times; and Coach Gray, who was a member of John Miller's mathematics department, got him through that situation.

At left:

Letter of commendation from Hazel Hibshman of Penn State, recognizing Don Robinson's successful first year as the head baseball coach at Bellefonte, when his 1964 team won the Central Penn League with an 8-0 record.

from the desk of
HAZEL HIBSHMAN

Hibshman was an avid football fan and a friend of Joe Bedenk, Robby's baseball coach at Penn State from 1960-62.

1964 District VI Baseball Tournament

As of May 25, Bert Williams, District 6 Baseball Tournament Director from Harmony High School, had received entries from the following schools: Curwensville, Bellefonte, Hollidaysburg, Lewistown, Richland Township, Portage, and Adams-Summerhill.

Bellefonte, the Central Penn League Champion with an 8-0 record, was originally scheduled to play Curwensville on May 25, but the Golden Tide's All-Sports Banquet took precedence. Bellefonte was then scheduled to play Hollidaysburg at Penn State's Beaver Field on May 26 at 5:30 p.m.

The Golden Tigers won the Blair County Scholastic League with a 10-0 record. Overall, they were 11-1, losing only to Altoona.

Bellefonte and Hollidaysburg met at Beaver Field on Tuesday, May 26; but the 4-4 game was called after 8 innings because of darkness.

The lead see-sawed back and forth until the 6th, when the Tigers scored a run and threatened to get more off starter Terry Perryman; but Coach Robinson called on sophomore Dave Whitehill with runners on first and second and one out, and he got the next two hitters to ground out.

In the top of the 7th, with Bellefonte up 4-3, Whitehill struck out the first two batters. Bobby Lawrence drew a walk after working a 3-2 count. He took second on a balk and raced home with the tying run on Ron Smith's single.

In the bottom of the 8th inning, Hollidaysburg's ace pitcher John Leamer, a lefty, walked Dave Whitehill and Dave Long. Coach Pat Cummings brought in another lefty, Dave Montrella, to pitch to Larry Conaway. After uncorking a wild pitch, Montrella intentionally walked Conaway to load the bases. Denny Lose, a left-handed hitter, took three straight balls but was fanned on a 3-2 count. On a delayed squeeze with Charlie Doland bunting, Whitehill was thrown out at the plate. Bellefonte's last hope, Ron Howard, lined to center to end the threat; and the umpires promptly called the game. The Raiders stranded three men in the fourth, sixth, and eighth innings.

At right: Larry "Hoppy" Conaway legs out a base hit in the third inning

43

The Bellefonte-Hollidaysburg re-match was scheduled for 1:45 on Tuesday, June 2, at Community Field in State College.

Coach Pat Cummings again went with his stopper John Leamer, while Coach Don Robinson called on Barry Burger, who responded by pitching seven strong innings with an effective curve ball, allowing only five hits.

The Tigers loaded the bases in the first inning, but Burger struck out the last two hitters to end the threat. In the 2nd, Burger again got out of a bases-loaded jam by retiring the last two hitters. Hollidaysburg went on top, 1-0 in the 3rd inning on three hits; but stranded two more runners.

Ron Howard

In the 4th, Larry Conaway hit a liner to center which bounced over Barry Kennedy's head and Conaway circled the bases, tying the game at 1.

Ron Hoover doubled to open the Tiger 6th, but Burger bore down and got an infield out along with two strikeouts to end the threat.

In the bottom of the 6th, with the game tied at 1-1, Leamer walked Larry Conaway, Denny Lose, and Charlie Doland. A visit to the mound by Coach Cummings resulted in Leamer staying in to face the next batter, Ron Howard, whom he had already retired twice. Howard jumped on the first pitch and hit it over the right fielder's head for a grand slam homer and a 5-1 Bellefonte lead. Prior to the blast, Leamer had allowed only 4 hits and struck out 9. Burger picked up his fifth win of the season.

Bellefonte, with a 9-0 record, met Lewistown, (12-4) in a semi-final district game at Community Field in State College on Friday, June 5. The Panthers of Coach Harry Johnson started Denny Drass, a junior southpaw; while Don Robinson countered with Dave Whitehill, a sophomore righty with a 2-0 regular season's record. Lewistown's starting lineup consisted of all underclassmen—in fact Johnson had only one senior on the team. Robinson's only lineup change found Terry Perryman in left field instead of Barry Hinds.

During practice on Thursday, June 4, Coach Gray was hitting infield during batting practice; and he drilled a liner that went over the shortstop's head. Unfortunately, right fielder Tom Bathgate was jogging across the infield on his way to batting practice and the ball hit him in the face, breaking his nose. His injury required a trip to the hospital, but Tom was in the starting lineup against Lewistown the next day with a face that looked like he had been in a prize fight.

44

On Friday, June 5, Robby's Raiders uncharacteristically committed five errors en route to a 7-5 loss to Lewistown, a team that eliminated Curwensville, 6-1, in order to reach the semi-finals.

Walks and errors were Bellefonte's downfall; but the Tribe battled back in the 7th inning, only to come up short.

The Panthers scored twice in the first on a hit batsman, a single, and a 2-base error. The Raiders tied the game in the second on a walk to Charlie Doland, a fielder's choice error, a 2-out single by Grant Lee and a passed ball.

Tom Bathgate

Lewistown went back on top 4-2 in the 3rd on two walks by losing pitcher Dave Whitehill and a 3-base throwing error.

In the 4th inning, Johnson's boys expanded their lead to 6-2. A single and two sacrifice bunt errors loaded the bases. Robinson brought in Barry Burger to pitch to Steve Ayres, who hit a sacrifice fly to center. A second run was the result of another Raider throwing error.

A single by Bob White accounted for Lewistown's final run in the 5th inning.

Bellefonte loaded the bases in the 6th, on a single and two walks; but could only muster one run on a sacrifice fly by Ron Howard.

Down 7-3, the Tribe rallied in the 7th and scored twice on a catcher's interference call, a single by pinch hitter Joe Menna, an infield out and a hit by Larry Conaway; but it wasn't enough, as the Panthers prevailed, 7-5.

Burger allowed only one run, one hit, and struck out four in his 3-inning stint. Lewistown's Denny Drass, who at one stage of the game retired 10 men in order, went the distance, giving up only four hits and striking out eight.

Lewistown won the District VI Title by defeating Adams-Summerhill, the defending champion, the following week in Altoona.

At left: Winning pitcher Barry Burger is mobbed after beating Hollidaysburg.

45

1965

Boys who played for Coach Robinson (left) and Coach Gray (right) in the 1965 season: Tom Bathgate, Barry Burger, Bill Shuey, Rich Yarnell, Barry Hinds, Terry Perryman, Leroy Smith, Fred Walker, Dave Whitehill, Frank Eckley, Dan Kustanbauter, Joe Menna, Steve McCulley, Gary Struble, Herb Beezer, Barry Perryman, Mel Harter, Jerry Luckovich, Bob O'Leary, Dan Leitzell, Gerald Hoy, Frank Menna, and Bill Bierly.

The top three pitchers in the Central Penn League in 1964 were Barry Burger (4-0); Terry Perryman (2-0); and Dave Whitehill (2-0). All three returned in 1965; but they had a young squad behind them and Whitehill was the only one able to win a ball game. He ended the season at 1-3, while Perryman and Burger combined for half the team's losses. Sophomore pitcher Dan Kustanbauter was 1-1 as the Raiders were 1-7 in the league and 2-8 overall.

The victories were: Lewistown (4-1) and State College (2-1). Losses came at the hands of: Lewistown (6-2); Penns Valley (8-7 & 14-7); State College (5-0); Philipsburg (2-0 & 8-2); and Bald Eagle (5-3 & 4-2).

After an opening season's loss to Lewistown at the Athletic Field in Bellefonte, the Tribe travelled to Lewistown for a rematch and was able to beat one of the Panther's best pitchers, right-left-hander[4] Barry Reinard, 4-1. He went the distance, giving up 4 runs on 7 hits with 4 free passes and 6 strikeouts. Terry Perryman had a double and an RBI for Bellefonte while Raider pitcher Dave Whitehill drove in two runs with a bases loaded two-bagger.

Whitehill yielded a run in the 3rd inning on a single, stolen base, an infield out, and another single. In 7 innings, he allowed 4 hits, 4 walks, and struck out 8 Panthers, four of them in the last two innings.

Upon returning to Bellefonte, the bus passed through town and the victorious Raiders yelled their lungs out through the pulled-down windows.

---

[4] Reinard was born with only a small thumb on his left hand and four stubs where his fingers should be. When he threw the baseball, his glove was tucked under his left arm; and would quickly switch it to his right hand to receive a return throw from the catcher or field a ball hit in his vicinity.

Dave Whitehill at the plate.

A Tribal Meeting breaks up.

Dan Kustanbauter pitched a one-hitter and Bellefonte defeated rival State College, 2-1, at Community Field in State College for its first league win.

The sophomore right-hander pitched 5 innings of hitless ball although the Little Lions put their run on the board in the 3rd. Denny Eminhizer reached base on an error, stole second, and moved to third on an infield out. A passed ball enabled Eminhizer to cross the plate.

Bellefonte, which had two seniors in the lineup (Terry Perryman and Tom Bathgate), scored in the first inning. Joe Menna singled and moved to second on Bathgate's sacrifice. Menna was erased at third on Gary Struble's grounder to pitcher Ralph Spearly. Struble promptly stole second, Barry Hinds walked, and a clutch single by Fred Walker plated Struble.

The Tribe took the lead in the 7th inning after two ground-outs. Terry Perryman walked and moved to third when Spearly threw Leroy Smith's grounder wildly to first base. Kustanbauter was hit by a pitch to load the bases; and Perryman scored on a wild pitch. Ed Temple relieved Spearly and got Joe Menna to ground out.

Bill Rudewick's single in the 6th spoiled Kustanbauter's no-hit bid; but he was thrown out trying to steal second by catcher Terry Perryman. After Larry Brown flied out, Ken Rhule walked; but Perryman nailed him trying to steal second to end the inning.

Left: Terry Perryman. Right: Leroy Smith at the plate.

47

In 1965 the Red Raiders were practicing after school in the high school gym on a day when it was too cold to be outside. A freshman catcher, Bruce Baney, was taking part in the workouts while the gym doors were open to the hallway. As the principal was leaving the building, he stopped at the gym door, looked in and saw Baney. He told Robby, "Tell that boy to get a haircut."

At that time, Beatlemania was sweeping the country, and Baney's hair style was similar to that of the Beatles. He refused to get a haircut, and quit the team. Robby wrote a letter to the School Board signed by both him and Coach Gray, asking that Baney be reinstated; but the board backed the principal.

Bruce Baney came out for the team the following year and his hair was no longer an issue. He was the starting catcher on three consecutive Central Penn League Championship teams in 1966-68.

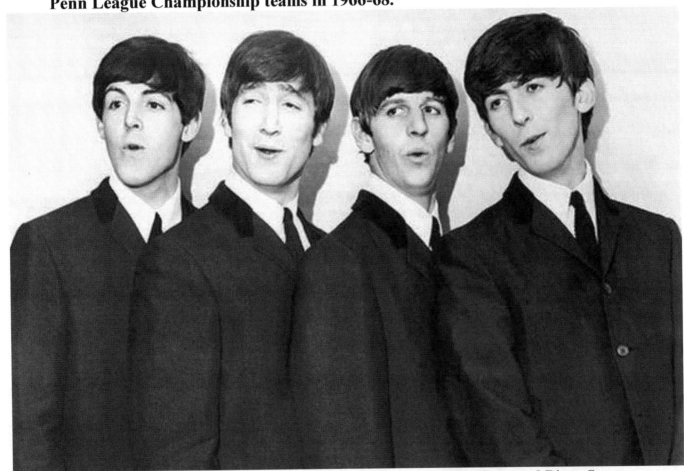

The Beatles, L-R: Paul McCartney, John Lennon, George Harrison, and Ringo Starr

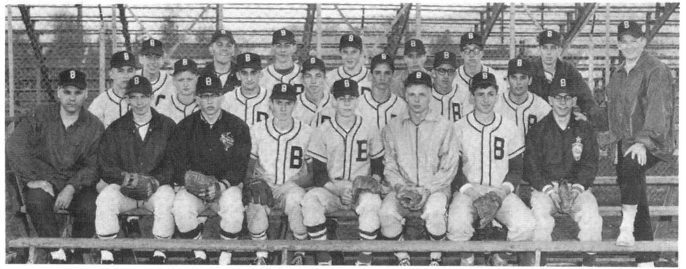

1966 Bellefonte High School Varsity Baseball Team
Central Penn League Champions

First Row, L-R: Assistant Coach Ralph Gray, Dan Kustanbauter, Barry Hinds, Rich Houser, Jack Aumiller, Sherman Lowry, Allen Ishler, Herb Beezer, Coach Don Robinson. **Row 2:** Gary Luckovich, Melvin Harter, Joe Menna, Dan Leitzell, Denny DeWitt, Frank Menna, Gary Struble. **Row 3:** Robert Miller, Bruce Baney, Barry Perryman, Gerald Hoy, Harold Gentzel, Fred Walker, Dave Whitehill.

The 1966 Red Raiders were 7-3 in the Central Penn League and 9-4 overall. Wins: Lewistown (8-5); Chief Logan (4-3); Penns Valley (12-2 & 10-3); State College (1-0); Lock Haven (9-4 &1-0); Philipsburg (6-2); Bald Eagle Area (2-1). Losses: Philipsburg (5-1); Bald Eagle Area (10-1); State College (8-4).

In District 6 competition, the Tribe lost in the first round to Clearfield, 17-8.

After a year in which the Raiders experienced some growing pains, they put it together in the 1966 season, winning the first of three consecutive Central Penn League Championships.

In the season's opener at Bellefonte, third baseman Fred Walker collected three hits, including a double and triple, and drove in three runs in an 8-5 victory over Lewistown.

Junior Dan Kustanbauter started on the mound for the Raiders, allowed only one hit, two runs, and struck out five in four innings of work. Sherm Lowry relieved in the 5th and gave up three runs on three hits while striking out four. Each Tribe pitcher issued three walks.

Bellefonte broke the game open in the third and took a 6-0 lead. Dan Leitzell started the rally with a single and moved to second on a single by Barry Hinds. Walker tripled and scored when Bruce Baney reached first on an error. Mel Harter and Kustanbauter singled, plating Baney, and Harter scored on a Joe Menna sacrifice. The Raiders batted around; and Leitzell's second hit was a home run; but he failed to touch second and got credit for a single.

The Panther's John Johnston had a two-run homer in the fourth inning.

The Red Raiders pulled off some 7th inning heroics at Bellefonte and knocked off Chief Logan, 4-3, for their second win.

Down 3-2 in the last inning, Bellefonte loaded the bases as Dan Leitzell and Dan Kustanbauter walked, and Joe Menna was hit by a pitch. Coach Robinson called for a triple steal, and Kustanbauter crossed the plate with the tying run. One out later, Barry Perryman drove home Menna to end the game.

The Mingoes took a 1-0 lead into the 2nd inning; but Bruce Baney's 2-run homer put the Raiders on top after Fred Walker had tripled.

Sherm Lowry went 5 innings, gave up 3 runs on 2 hits while walking 3 and striking out 5. Kustanbauter pitched the last two innings and got the win. He struck out the side both times while allowing one free pass.

Three of the Raider's four hits were for extra bases including a Dave Whitehill triple.

At the Athletic Field in Bellefonte, the Raiders greeted Central Penn League newcomer Lock Haven rudely with a 9-4 victory. The visitors were coached by Joe Danis. Despite the cold weather, pitcher Dave Whitehill pitched a 3-hitter, walked 3, and struck out 11 Bobcats in his 7 innings, while picking up his first win.

Bellefonte jumped out to a 3-0 lead in the 3rd inning on singles by Whitehill and Joe Menna, an error, and Gary Struble's opposite-field single.

After Lock Haven tied the score in the fourth, the Tribe went up 9-3 in their half of the inning. Jerry Luckovich led off with a double, followed by a pinch-hit by Jack Aumiller, a Menna single, walks to Dan Leitzell, Struble, and Barry Hinds, a hit-batsman, and a wild pitch. The six tallies doomed Danis' Bobcats.

Centerfielder Joe Menna made a great play in the 6th, throwing out Lock Haven's Lininger at third base, limiting the Bobcats to one run in the inning.

Bellefonte's Dan Kustanbauter picked up his second win of the season by going 6 innings against Penns Valley, holding the Rams to 2 hits, 2 runs, and striking out 6. Sherm Lowry mopped up and pitched no-hit, no-run, baseball.

The Raiders roughed up three Penns Valley hurlers for 12 hits and 12 runs and improved their record to 4-0. Dan Leitzell and Fred Walker both tripled and led the assault with 2 hits each, driving in 5 runs. Dave Whitehill drove in 2 runs, while Bruce Baney, Barry Hinds, and Kustanbauter plated one each.

Kustanbauter had a no-hitter going into the 6th inning at Millheim; but Coach Robinson felt he was tiring, so he inserted Lowry, allowing him to gain experience in relief.

Coach Jack McMullen's Rams committed eleven errors in the 12-4 loss.

The Raiders had two miscues and took over first place in the Central Penn League with a 2-0 record.

Bellefonte played errorless baseball at Community Field in State College and extended its record in the league to 3-0, one game ahead of Bald Eagle Area. Raider right-hander Dave Whitehill pitched a gem, shutting out the Little Lions on 3 hits, allowing only one free pass, and striking out eight for his second win.

Ralph Spearly held the visitors to 4 hits; and Joe Menna had three of them in the 1-0 Raider victory.

However, the Tribe won the game in the 6th inning, scoring a run without a hit. Gary Struble led off and reached first on an error. He promptly stole second (one of 6 Raider thefts in the game), and moved to third on a wild pitch. Spearly then struck out the next batter, and got Fred Walker to line out to short. Bruce Baney had a 3-2 count on him but the next pitch went into the dirt and bounced away from catcher Bill Cloninger, allowing Struble to score standing up.

Only one Little Lion reached second base, that being in the third inning. Meanwhile, the Raiders threatened in the first inning on a single by Joe Menna, a one-out hit by Struble, who advanced to second on the State College outfield relay. A foul out and a grounder to third ended a great opportunity for the Tribe to put a number on the board.

Philipsburg-Osceola's Fred Covey limited Bellefonte to one run on 3 hits, while striking out 12 at the Athletic Field for a 5-1 victory. According to Coach Don Robinson, Covey was the best pitcher in the league, and the loss should take the pressure off his unbeaten Tribe.

The Mounties took a 1-0 lead in the top of the first and added 3 more in the 3rd.

Bellefonte averted a shutout in the fourth inning when Gary Struble and Barry Hinds singled with one out, putting runners on first and third. Fred Walker's grounder forced Hinds at second, scoring Struble. A walk to Bruce Baney was followed by a strikeout, thus ending the threat.

Philipsburg tacked on an insurance run in the fifth on a two-out single by Harry Townsend.

Covey picked a Raider runner off first in the first inning and retired the last eight batters he faced.

Dan Kustanbauter absorbed the loss, allowing four runs, two hits, four free passes, and struck out one Mountie in his three innings pitched.

In relief, Sherm Lowry gave up one run, three hits, two walks, and struck out two. Dave Whitehill pitched no-hit ball in the last inning and put a zero on the board while striking out two.

In 1966, the Bellefonte Junior Varsity beat State College at Pine Grove Mills, 2-1; Penns Valley at Bellefonte, 12-0; lost to Philipsburg 6-2 at Bellefonte and Bald Eagle, 2-1 at Unionville.

First place in the Central Penn League was at stake when Bellefonte (3-1) travelled to Wingate to take on a very good Bald Eagle team, also at 3-1.

Everything seemed to go wrong for the Raiders, who were limited to 5 singles (Joe Menna had two) by Eagle pitcher Terry Yearick, and committed an uncharacteristic seven errors in the 10-1 loss.

Bald Eagle, with seven left-handed hitters in the lineup, touched up three right-handed Raider pitchers for 8 hits and 10 runs. Dave Whitehill took the loss, giving up 6 runs, 4 hits, 3 walks, and struck out one batter in his 2-inning stint. Dan Kustanbauter relieved in the third; but Doc Etters' crew added 2 more runs on 2 hits. Six Eagles were struck out by Kustanbauter in his 3 innings pitched. Sherm Lowry pitched the final frame; but the Eagles kept their offense going by scoring 2 runs on 2 hits. Bob Stonebraker, John Yecina, and Cordy Chambers led the Eagle hit parade with two safeties each.

Bald Eagle took a 1-0 lead in the first inning; but the Tribe tied the score in their half of the second. Fred Walker led off with a single, and after a wild pitch, Yearick retired the next two hitters. Frank Menna delivered a clutch single to score Walker with the tying run.

The Eagles batted around in the second inning, and put the game out of reach.

Bellefonte snapped a 2-game losing streak by drubbing Penns Valley 10-3 at the Athletic Field on Tuesday, May 3. Dan Kustanbauter (2-1) got the win.

The Rams took a 1-0 lead in the first inning as Frank Slenker walked and Dave Marshall reached on a bunt single. Outfielder Frank Menna made a diving catch of a Marty Ilgen fly ball; but Slenker, who had tagged up at second base, was called out for leaving the bag too soon. Kustanbauter then hit Ron Stover and Scott Vogt, loading the bases; and a walk to Denny Bressler forced in a run.

In the bottom of the 2nd, Ram starter Ilgen walked Fred Walker, who moved to third on a Frank Menna double. Dave Whitehill singled for a 2-1 Raider lead.

The Rams tied the score in the third on an Ilgen double and a Vogt single.

Bellefonte grabbed a 4-2 lead in its half of the 3rd thanks to a walk to Gary Struble and two Ram errors.

The Raiders added two more runs in the fifth on walks to Struble and Barry Hinds, a Walker single, and another Ram miscue.

In the sixth inning, Penns Valley loaded the bases; and Coach Robinson called on senior pitcher Whitehill, who put out the fire, allowing only one run.

The Tribe batted around in the 6th, and scored four more runs. Joe Menna walked, singles by Dan Leitzell and pinch-hitter Denny DeWitt , an error, two walks, and a single by Jack Aumiller ended the scoring.

Bellefonte had six hits to the Rams' five. The game was marred by 16 walks and 6 errors. Ilgen (2-1) went 5 innings and struck out 6.

On Wednesday, May 4, Bellefonte topped Lock Haven, 1-0 on the road and stayed atop the Central Penn League standings.

Dave Whitehill (3-1) pitched a 2-hitter, walked one, and struck out seven. Bobcat Bill Bowes had a double in the second and Mike Boone had an infield single in the sixth inning. At one point he retired nine 'Cats in a row.

Jerry Hanley (0-3) pitched a 4-hitter and struck out 12. At one stretch he retired 10 Raiders in a row, and another time retired 6 men in order.

Hanley walked Joe Menna to start the game. Menna stole second and scored on a single by Dan Leitzell to right field.

In the second inning, Bill Bechdel reached on an error and Bowes followed with a double. A relay from Joe Menna-to Leitzell-to Bruce Baney nailed Bechdel at the plate. Raider catcher Baney also threw out two runners at second.

In the bottom of the seventh, Whitehill issued a one-out walk, but the Tribe turned a double play, ending the game.

Struble led the Tribe in hits with two; and Fred Walker also singled.

At a wind-blown Athletic Field on Friday, May 6, State College got revenge from an earlier 1-0 defeat by beating Bellefonte, 8-4.

State moved out to a 1-0 lead in the first inning when Ralph Spearly drilled a Sherm Lowry pitch to deep center for a home run.

The Little Lions made it 6-0 in the third on a Rich Pierce single, a sacrifice-fielder's choice, a Jim Wagner single, a hit batsman, a squeeze bunt by Leon Slick, a double by Stan Wilson, and an error.

State College went up 8-0 in the fourth on an error, singles by Jerry Ross, Wagner, John Swanger, and Slick.

The Raiders got on the board in the fourth on a Gary Struble single, a 3-base error, and singles by Bruce Baney and Barry Hinds. Coach Bob Smith brought in Spearly to relieve Wagner and the senior right-hander got Barry Perryman on strikes and Joe Menna on a pop fly to first.

Lowry (0-1) allowed 6 runs on 5 hits and struck out 2 Lions in his two and two-thirds innings of work. Joe Menna in relief, allowed 8 hits, 2 runs, and struck out 4 the rest of the way. The Raider pitchers did not walk a batter.

The Raiders had seven singles. Hinds had two RBI's and pinch-hitter Denny Dewitt drove in one with a single.

Wagner only pitched three and a third innings, so he did not qualify for the win (A starting pitcher must go four innings in a seven inning game). Spearly (3-2) went three and two-thirds, allowing only two hits and one run.

Coach Bob Smith's Little Lions lost their first four games by one run.

Bellefonte kept pace with league-leading Bald Eagle with a big 6-2 win at Philipsburg; setting up a game with the Eagles the next day at Bellefonte which would decide the Central Penn Championship.

The Raiders wasted no time, putting two runs on the board in the first inning. Joe Menna reached base on a bunt single. After a wild pitch by losing pitcher Dan Danko, a lefty, Dan Leitzell singled home Menna. An infield out, a passed ball, a hit batsman (Barry Hinds), and a sacrifice fly by Fred Walker plated Leitzell.

The Tribe increased its lead to 5-0 in the third inning on Joe Menna's infield hit, a fielder's choice, a Gary Struble single, an infield hit by Barry Hinds, a Walker single, a hit batsman (Frank Menna), and a bases-loaded walk to Bruce Baney.

The final Raider run was scored in the fourth inning on Joe Menna's third hit, a stolen base, and two Mountie miscues.

Philipsburg scored its two runs in the bottom of the fourth on two singles, an infield out, and a 2-run error. Bellefonte committed only 2 errors in the game.

Raider pitcher Dave Whitehill ran his record to 4-1 in the league, tying Terry Yearick of Bald Eagle. Whitehill retired the first eight batters in order, gave up only 3 hits, walked 4, and struck out 7 in going the distance.

Hinds had 2 hits, as did Walker, who drove in 3 runs.

Joe Menna, a left-hander, skipped the Bellefonte junior class trip to Gettysburg along with teammate Gary Struble and engaged in a 10-inning pitching battle with southpaw Terry Yearick of Bald Eagle at the Bellefonte Athletic Field.

The Raiders had a runner in scoring position in the first inning with one out; but Yearick struck out the next hitter and got the final out on a foul pop-up.

Etters' Eagles failed to score in the second inning despite a single followed by a triple. An attempted sacrifice bunt was popped up and caught by third baseman Fred Walker, who doubled up the runner on first, who had singled. John Simpson followed with a triple, but Menna retired the final batter on a ground-out

The Eagles scored their only run in the fourth inning on a leadoff double by Bob Stonebraker, an infield hit by Cordy Chambers, and John Yecina's infield out. A base hit by Terry Simpson and a Dave Walker walk loaded the bases; but Menna got Yearick to pop out to Fred Walker at third.

The Tribe came right back and tied the game at one on a Walker single, a walk to Dave Whitehill, and a single by Bruce Baney.

Menna allowed only one hit over the last 5 innings that being a Stonebraker single in the 8th.

Yearick, meanwhile, had a 3-hitter going into the 10th inning and had retired 16 men in a row at one stretch. Whitehill led off the 10th with a double; and a one-out single by freshman Denny DeWitt broke the tie, giving Bellefonte its second Central Penn Title in 3 years.

In 1966 Bellefonte had an important Central Penn League game with Bald Eagle Area at the Athletic Field in Bellefonte. The field was a mess; but the Tribe wanted to play that day because the Eagles' best pitcher, Terry Yearick (5-1) would be pitching with short rest. It took a lot of work to get the field playable, and every flake of sawdust that the high school wood shop could spare was utilized in soaking up the moisture on the grounds.

Bald Eagle's Coach Doc Etters wasn't happy to see the condition of the field; but he had his ace Yearick ready to go and a talented lineup that had seven left-handed batters that hammered the Raider right-handed pitchers in the first meeting of the two squads.

Robby countered Yearick with outfielder Joe Menna, who at times pitched batting practice; and the crafty, sneaky-fast lefty kept the Eagles off balance. Menna's strong performance, along with some timely hitting and great defense, enabled the Raiders to win their second Central Penn League Title. Joe Menna was Bellefonte's leadoff hitter and Yearick's first pitch hit him on the helmet; but he was not hurt, and pitched the game of his life.

Bellefonte's Denny DeWitt is carried off the field following his walk off hit.

Coach Don Robinson's brother Jay Robinson had Joe Menna in his English Composition Class at Bellefonte High School; and he knew Joe was going to pitch in the championship game against Bald Eagle. He told Menna if he pitched well and won the game, he would give him an "A" in his last composition of the year. Needless to say, Joe got an "A".

District VI Playoff

Clearfield, the Moshannon Valley League champion, walloped Bellefonte in a 3-hour first round playoff game at Philipsburg, 17-8.

The Bison jumped on Raider starter Dave Whitehill in the first inning, scoring seven runs on 4 hits and 3 walks. Whitehill struck out one batter.

At left: A Clearfield runner scores in the first inning at Philipsburg. The Bellefonte catcher is sophomore Bruce Baney.

Dan Kustanbauter took the hill in the second inning; and in his two and a third innings, allowed 9 runs on 2 hits and 6 walks, striking out 5. Jerry Luckovich finished the third inning and went one more, giving up Clearfield's final run on two hits and one walk, while striking out one. Joe Menna mopped up for Bellefonte, allowing 2 hits and one walk in his one inning of work. He struck out two Bison batters.

In the first inning, the Raiders had a chance to break the game open; but had to settle for three runs. Clearfield pitcher Larry Stiner's strikeout with the bases loaded ended the inning in which he walked four and allowed singles by Fred Walker and Bruce Baney.

The Bison came right back in the bottom of the first, scoring 6 runs on 4 hits, a walk, and 4 Bellefonte errors. The Raiders had 9 miscues in the contest.

In the third inning, Steve Norris belted a 3-run homer and teammate Ed Howell followed with a grand-slam homer in the fourth for Clearfield.

Bellefonte had seven hits in the game and scored eight runs; but could not overcome the offensive power of Clearfield.

Coach Don Robinson cleared his bench, giving all of his boys some playing time in the last game of the season.

The father of a Bellefonte player came to every game and sat in the bleachers behind the team bench. He was rather vocal about his son. On one occasion, the boy reached first base and shortly after stole second. Coaches Robinson and Gray looked at each other, and Robby asked, "Did you give him the steal signal?" Gray replied, "No, did you?" Robby then said, "His dad must have given him a steal signal."

1966 Bellefonte Junior Varsity Baseball Team[5]

First Row, L-R: Jerry Yarnell, Don Lucas, Bob O'Leary, Jim Walker, Jerry Walker, Mike Kelleher. **Row 2:** Ray Fisher, Phil Diehl, Denny Ebeling, Keith Haney, Joe Krall. **Row 3:** Coach Ralph Gray, Jerry Glenn, Tom Knoffsinger, Sam Nastase, Frank Oesterling.

Also, in 1966, Bellefonte boys, ages 13-15, were Pennsylvania State VFW Teener League Champions. Picture was taken in Miffllintown after the final win.
First Row, L-R: Dave O'Shell**, Denny Ebeling*, Jim Grey**, Jerry Glenn*, Herb Beezer*.
Row 2: State Tournament Director George Caba, Ray Fisher*, Bob O'Leary*, Denny DeWitt*, Dan Leitzell*, Sam Nastase*, Frank Oesterling*, Jeff Watson*. **Row 3:** Coach Les McClellan, Glenn Hinds*, Jim Hoy*, George Confer*, John Wetzler* Manager Dick Leathers, League Treasurer Dick Bartlett, VFW Official.   ***Player   **Alternate**

---

[5] First JV Team in Bellefonte History

1967 Bellefonte High School Varsity Baseball Team

First Row, L-R: Manager John Rockey, Keith Haney, Dan Leitzell, Sam Nastase, Jerry Luckovich, Herb Beezer, Denny DeWitt, Joe Menna, Denny Ebeling, Bob O'Leary. **Row 2:** Assistant Coach Ralph Gray, Gary Struble, Frank Oesterling, Jack Aumiller, Dan Kustanbauter, Mel Harter, Frank Menna, Bruce Baney, Tom Purnell, Bob Walker, Don Lucas, Coach Don Robinson.

The Red Raiders had seven lettermen returning from last year's Central Penn League Championship Team: Bruce Baney, Gary Struble, Danny Leitzell, Joe Menna, Dan Kustanbauter, Jack Aumiller, and Frank Menna. Kustanbauter and Joe Menna were two of the four seniors on the team.

Key losses by graduation were: Dave Whitehill, Barry Hinds, and Fred Walker.

About 75 candidates reported for indoor drills in March. Coach Don Robinson will keep 22 on the varsity and the remaining players will be under the direction of Assistant Ralph Gray, the junior varsity coach.

For the second year in a row, the Red Raiders won the Central Penn League. Their league record was 8-2; and overall was 8-5.

Central Penn League: Wins—Lock Haven (3-1 & 7-1); Penns Valley (6-4 & 12-1); State College (6-1 & 4-0); and Philipsburg (5-4 & 1-0). Losses— Bald Eagle (4-3 & 4-3).

The Raiders lost both exhibition games—Lewistown (3-2) and Bishop Guilfoyle (5-4).

In District VI competition, Bellefonte was eliminated in the first round by Clearfield, 5-4.

1967 Junior Varsity results: Wins—Penns Valley (13-0 & 19-3); State College (7-2); and Bald Eagle Area (12-2). Loss—State College (5-4).

The Red Raiders opened the 1967 season on April 7 at Lewistown and came out on the short end of a 3-2 score.

Bellefonte got on the board in the first inning after Joe Menna and Gary Struble got free passes from starter Breon, putting runners on first and second. Dan Leitzell's grounder forced Struble at second. Leitzell then got in a run-down and Menna raced home with the game's first score.

The Panthers made it 2-1 in their half of the inning on two singles, a walk, and a sacrifice.

The Tribe tied the game in the 2nd frame. Denny DeWitt opened with a walk from reliever Lepley and took second on a wild pitch. A walk to Jerry Luckovich was followed by a strikeout; and a walk to Bob O'Leary loaded the bases. Pitcher Dan Kustanbauter then drove in DeWitt with a broken-bat single.

Lewistown squeezed across a run in the third inning and held on for the win.

Joe Menna had two of the Raider's five hits; and starter Kustanbauter allowed 4 hits, 3 runs, one walk, and struck out 4 in his three innings.

Leitzell took the hill in the fourth and pitched no-hit ball in two innings of relief, striking out two Panthers. Joe Menna mopped up and did not allow a hit in his one inning while striking out two.

At Lock Haven on Tuesday, April 11, Bellefonte got its first win of the season thanks to Tom Purnell's two-run double in the 8th inning.

Bellefonte scored once in the 4th inning on an error, a Dan Leitzell single, and a two-out error. Gary Struble got aboard on an error; and after Leitzell's hit, starter Hal Shady retired the next two batters on pop-ups. Bruce Baney's grounder was booted, and Struble scored.

The Raider lead held up until the sixth when Rod Kodish hit Dan Kustanbauter's first pitch over the right field fence, knotting the score at 1-1.

Leitzell started the eighth inning rally with a one-out single. Coach Joe Danis called in Kodish from first base to pitch to Sam Nastase; but the lefty hit Nastase on the foot. Purnell's second double went to the fence, putting Coach Don Robinson's Raiders on top, 3-1.

Kustanbauter (1-0) went the distance, giving up five hits, one run, and one walk, while striking out 12. He retired the Bobcats in order in the bottom of the eighth.

Losing pitcher Shady (0-1) allowed three hits, two runs, two walks, and struck out seven Raiders. Leitzell and Purnell had four of Bellefonte's five hits.

A strong Tribe defense contributed to the 3-1 victory. Bruce Baney threw out a runner at second in the first inning, and made a one-handed stab on a pop-up in the third. Great defensive plays by Baney, Kustanbauter, and Struble in the fourth inning got the Raiders out of a bases-loaded jam.

Bellefonte improved its Central Penn record to 2-0 on Friday, April 14, against Penns Valley at the Athletic Field with a 6-4 victory.

The game was decided in the first inning. The visiting Rams jumped out to a 2-0 lead after junior right-hander Dan Leitzell had retired the first two hitters. Roger Wert singled, moved to second on a wild pitch and scored on a home run by Jan Millon.

Leadoff hitter Joe Menna walked to start the bottom of the inning and scored on a Gary Struble triple. Ram pitcher Gary Smith struck out the next batter; but Struble scored on a ground-out by Sam Nastase. Tom Purnell promptly homered, breaking a 2-2 tie. Bruce Baney followed with a single, and second baseman Jerry Luckovich homered, making the score 5-2. Umpire Lloyd Sorrels ruled that centerfielder Sanford Nevel had trapped Baney's fly ball; and Penns Valley Coach Ed Drapcho argued to no avail.

Leitzell settled down and limited the Rams to one hit in the second and a walk to Fred Stover in the fourth. Eight of his 12 strikeouts were in the first 4 frames.

The Tribe made it 6-2 in the fourth. Joe Menna walked, stole second, and scored on a Struble single.

Penns Valley added a run in the fifth after two outs. An error, a single, and a wild pitch plated the tally. A free pass followed; but a strikeout ended the inning.

With one out in the 7th, a walk and error put Ram runners on first and second. Leitzell was able to get a force out at second on a grounder; but a run scored on a slow grounder by the next hitter. Leitzell (1-0) struck out the final batter.

A strong pitching performance by Dan Kustanbauter and clutch hitting by Robby's Raiders enabled them to move into first place with a 6-1 victory over rival State College at the Athletic Field in Bellefonte on Tuesday, April 18.

Bellefonte scored two runs in the first off losing pitcher Jim Wagner on a walk to Joe Menna, a double by Gary Struble, a wild pitch, and a delayed steal in which Dan Leitzell was retired in a rundown.

The Red Raiders made it 5-0 in the second inning. Jerry Luckovich walked and was sacrificed to second by Frank Menna. Kustanbauter then bunted Luckovich to third. Joe Menna singled home Luckovich, stole second, and came home on a Struble double. Leitzell then singled, and another delayed steal enabled Struble to cross the plate before Leitzell was tagged out in a rundown.

Kustanbauter (2-0) had a no-hitter for four and two-thirds innings. He struck out 8, but surrendered a run in the fifth after two outs as the Little Lions recorded their only hits (2 singles) and one of three total walks.

Bellefonte added an insurance run in the sixth on a two-out single by Joe Menna and Herb Beezer's triple. Joe Menna, Struble, Sam Nastase, and Kustanbauter each had two hits for the winners, who touched up Wagner for eleven safeties.

Bald Eagle Area made the most of five hits and three Bellefonte errors to beat the Red Raiders 4-3 at the Athletic Field on Tuesday, April 25. With the win, the Eagles took over the first spot in the Central Penn League at 4-0 while the Tribe fell to 3-1.

In the bottom of the first inning, Bellefonte took a 1-0 lead. Southpaw Cordy Chambers yielded a double to Joe Menna, who raced to third on an Eagle error. After two hitters had been retired, Sam Nastase singled home Menna.

Coach Doc Etters' boys put three runs on the board in the third. John Simpson got a free pass from starter Dan Kustanbauter (2-1), and Gary Bartley's sacrifice bunt was blooped over first baseman Tom Purnell's head. The ball was fielded by the second baseman who threw it by the shortstop into the outfield. Kustanbauter retired the next two hitters, but a single by Kim Kunes plated two runners. Two more walks loaded the bases, then Kustanbauter hit Denny Kolasa, forcing in the third tally.

In their half of the third, the Raiders tied the score on a walk to Joe Menna, a Herb Beezer bingle, a Dan Leitzell sacrifice, and a Nastase two-run single.

Bald Eagle broke the 3-3 tie in the fourth frame. Leading off, Simpson singled and moved to second on a Bartley sacrifice. Craig Alterio hit a grounder to short and Simpson scored when Leitzell's throw was dropped at home plate.

Joe Menna pitched the last two innings, gave up one hit and struck out three.

The win seemed to boost the confidence of the Eagles, who had lost important games to Bellefonte in each of the last two seasons.

Chambers (2-0) allowed six hits and four walks to the Tribe; but the Raider defensive mistakes were costly. Coach Don Robinson hoped his squad got everything out of its system and would play Bellefonte baseball the rest of the way.

On Friday, April 28, Bellefonte began a five-game winning streak by topping Lock Haven, 7-1, at the Athletic Field. The Raiders banged out nine hits off Bobcat pitchers Ron Kodish and Mike Packer and collected five free passes. Kodish (1-1) went two innings and absorbed the loss.

In the bottom of the first, Joe Menna led off with a single, and a one-out homer by Dan Leitzell staked the Tribe to a 2-0 advantage.

Pitcher Dan Kustanbauter's one-out triple and a sacrifice fly by Joe Menna upped the Raider lead to 3-0 in the second inning.

Bellefonte added two runs in the third off reliever Packer, making the score 5-0.

In the fourth frame, a Joe Menna double, two walks, and a hit batsman gave Coach Don Robinson's Raiders a 6-1 lead.

Dan Kustanbauter (3-1) went the distance, yielding one run on five hits, one walk, and struck out seven. He was two for two at the plate and scored two runs.

At Philipsburg on Saturday, April 29, Bellefonte tied Bald Eagle Area for first place in the Central Penn League with a 5-4 victory over the Mounties.

The Raiders spotted the home team a 4-0 lead, then scored two in the fourth and three more in the fifth.

In the fourth frame, a double by Sam Nastase, a single by Tom Purnell, a walk to Bruce Baney and sacrifice flies by Frank Menna and Mel Harter cut the Mountie lead in half.

The Tribe went on top in the fifth on a single by Gary Struble, a walk to Dan Leitzell, a single by Nastase, and a Joe Menna triple.

Joe Menna started for the Raiders and went three and a third innings, giving up five hits, four runs, and two walks, while striking out one.

Leitzell (2-0) went the rest of the way and picked up the win. He yielded only one hit and struck out one Mountie.

Purnell and Nastase had five of the Tribe's eight hits.

Coach Gerry Davis went with Dan Danko (3-1), who relinquished eight hits, five runs, walked two, and struck out five in seven innings. The lefty had a good day at the plate with three hits, including two doubles.

On Wednesday, May 3, Bellefonte took sole possession of first place in the CPL with a 12-1 thrashing of Penns Valley at Spring Mills. The Raiders pounded out 13 hits and were aided by six walks and six errors. The Tribe played errorless baseball.

The visitors wasted no time, jumping on Ram starter Millon in the first inning. A three-run homer by Denny DeWitt and a solo blast by Tom Purnell put the Raiders on top, 4-0.

Leading by 6-0, Bellefonte added three more in the fifth to clinch the victory. Purnell had four hits in the contest and Joe Menna and Gary Struble chipped in with two each. DeWitt and Bruce Baney combined for eight runs-batted-in.

Dan Leitzell (3-0) started on the hill, and yielded five hits, one run, two walks, and struck out three in five innings of work.

Joe Menna, in relief, allowed no runs on two hits, one walk, and struck out four in his two innings.

Bob Snyder had two of Penns Valley's seven hits.

Coach Don Robinson cleared his bench as the Red Raiders tuned up for an important game at State College on Friday.

In a fast-moving game at Community Field in State College, Bellefonte beat State College, 4-1, on Friday, May 5. The first basemen combined for 17 putouts in a contest that took one hour and 20 minutes and featured numerous ground balls. One more win would give Bellefonte its second consecutive CPL Title.

The Raiders scored once in the first inning off starter Corky Carter on singles by Gary Struble, Dan Leitzell, and Sam Nastase.

In the fifth, Jerry Luckovich opened the inning with a single and scored on Struble's second hit.

State scored its only run in the sixth off Raider pitcher Dan Kustanbauter on a one-out single by Denny Rhule, who moved to third on a throwing error and scored on a sacrifice fly by Chuck Fedon.

The Tribe made it 4-1 in the seventh. Luckovich stroked a one-out double to right, Kustanbauter was hit by a pitch, and a Joe Menna single loaded the bases. Struble's third hit plated two runs; but Menna was thrown out at home on a relay from Fedon-to Rhule-to Mike Houser.

Kustanbauter (4-1) was masterful on the mound, yielding only three hits, one run, and striking out eight. He did not allow a walk in his seven innings.

Moriarta relieved Carter in the seventh and got the final out. Carter (1-I) was touched up for nine Bellefonte hits and struck out one batter.

Each team committed only one error in a well-played game.

The Raiders of Coach Don Robinson won their third Central Penn League Title in four years on Wednesday, May 10, at the Athletic Field with a 1-0 victory over Philipsburg-Osceola.

Dan Leitzell (4-0) was the pitching and batting star and continued his mastery of the Mounties. He beat Philipsburg in the 1966 Pennsylvania State VFW Teener Tournament en route to the Bellefonte All-Stars' State Championship.

In the third, the leadoff hitter for Bellefonte singled, but was picked off first by lefty Dan Danko (4-2). Leitzell followed with a triple and scored on an infield out by Joe Menna. Danko scattered five hits, walked one, and struck out seven.

In the second inning, Philipsburg moved a runner to second via a sacrifice; but Leitzell retired the next two hitters. With one out in the fifth, Danko doubled with one out; but Leitzell whiffed the remaining batters. He had 7 strikeouts on the day.

In the bottom of the 2nd, Tom Purnell singled but was erased on a double play.

Sam Nastase singled with one out in the fourth inning, but a strikeout and an infield out stranded him at first.

Nastase singled again in the sixth, but was thrown out at second trying to stretch the hit into a double.

Leitzell did not allow a runner past second in pitching a nifty 3-hitter, and issued only one free pass. Each team committed one error in a well-played game.

At Unionville on Tuesday, May 16, Bald Eagle defeated the Red Raiders, 4-3, in an eight-inning contest.

Bellefonte moved out to a 3-0 lead off winning pitcher John Simpson (3-0); but the Eagles tied the score in the third inning, the big blow being Kim Kunes' solo home run.

In the eighth inning, Cordy Chambers singled off reliever Dan Kustanbauter (4-2). An error and Craig Alterio's sacrifice put runners on second and third. Coach Doc Etters called for a squeeze bunt with Denny Kolasa at bat; and it was executed perfectly, as Chambers came home with the winning run.

In eight innings of work, Simpson yielded only four singles, three runs, and struck out six Raiders. He did not walk a batter.

Joe Menna started on the mound for Bellefonte and went three and a third innings. He gave up five hits, three runs, two walks, and struck out four.

Kustanbauter relinquished four hits, one run, and struck out three Eagles. He did not allow any free passes.

On May 18, Bishop Guilfoyle defeated Bellefonte in a non-league game at Altoona, 5-4. Dan Leitzell was the losing pitcher and Joe Menna had half of the Raider's four hits. Winning pitcher Stover went the final three innings, not allowing a hit or run. He walked one batter and struck out none. Leitzell gave up five hits, five runs, walked five, and struck out four in six innings.

Dan Leitzell

Battery of Dan Kustanbauter and Bruce Baney

For the second straight year, Clearfield eliminated Bellefonte in the first round of the District 6 Playoffs; this time by a 5-4 margin on May 31 at Philipsburg.

The Bison took advantage of three costly Raider errors; and some clutch pitching by starter and winner Gary Leigley and reliever Bill Billotte.

In the first inning, Bellefonte jumped out to a short-lived 2-0 lead when Dan Leitzell tripled home Bruce Baney and Bob O'Leary.

Clearfield came right back in the next inning and tied the game on an error and two singles. Billotte's bingle drove in two runs.

The Tribe went ahead, 3-2, in the fourth frame as Gary Struble crossed the plate on a delayed steal.

Clearfield made it 4-3 in the fifth with a walk, two singles, and an error. One run was scored on a delayed steal and another on Steve Norris' RBI single.

The Bison added on in the seventh inning on a single by Billotte and he scored on a single by Bob Helm when the Raider outfielder bobbled the ball.

Down 5-3 with two outs in the seventh, Sam Nastase drew a walk. Tom Purnell promptly tripled, making the score 5-4. Billotte was called in from left field to squelch the rally, and he did just that, by striking out the last hitter.

Leitzell absorbed the tough loss, going seven innings, yielding five runs, seven hits, three walks, and striking out four.

Leitzell was three for three at the plate.

Bald Eagle Area's Gary Bartley, who hailed from Port Matilda, was a student-volunteer assistant to Chuck Medlar at Penn State; then became the University of North Carolina Charlotte's first baseball coach in 1979. After leaving the 49ers, he took the head baseball job at Lock Haven University where he completed his coaching career.

January 23—Stan Musial named General Manager of the St. Louis Cardinals.

April 20—Tom Seaver earned his first major league victory over the Cubs.

May 14—Mickey Mantle hit his 500th home run, batting left-handed.

June 7—Willie Stargell hit his 100th career home run.

World Series: The St. Louis Cardinals beat the Boston Red Sox, 4-3.

College World Series Champion: Arizona State.

Little League World Champion: West Tokyo, Japan.

1968 Bellefonte High School Varsity Baseball Team
Central Penn League Champions and District VI Champions
First Row, L-R: Frank Menna, Herb Beezer, Don Lucas. **Row 2:** Denny Ebeling, Bill Bierly, Denny DeWitt, Sam Nastase, Tom Purnell, Bruce Baney, Keith Haney, Frank Nolan. **Row 3:** Coach Don Robinson, Melvin Harter, Jerry Luckovich, Jeff Watson, Tom Knoffsinger, Dan Leitzell, Bob O'Leary, Dave O'Shell, Manager Bob Wallace.

The 1968 Red Raider baseball team had the following boys from the 1966 Bellefonte team that won the State VFW Teener Championship: Dave O'Shell, Denny Ebeling, Herb Beezer, Bob O'Leary, Denny DeWitt, Dan Leitzell, Sam Nastase, and Jeff Watson.

Ten lettermen were among the 17 candidates that Coach Don Robinson was working with. Key losses from graduation included Joe Menna, Gary Struble, and Dan Kustanbauter.

Assistant Coach Ralph Gray was working with a junior varsity squad of 25 players.

The 1968 Red Raiders were 10-0 in winning the Central Penn League Championship for the third straight season; and finished with a 15-1 record for the year, which included their first District VI Title.

Central Penn League wins: Lock Haven (27-1 & 1-0); Penns Valley (13-1 & 10-5); State College (3-2 & 6-2); Philipsburg (1-0 & 6-2); Bald Eagle (5-0 & 4-3).

Non-league games: Wins—Lewistown (2-1) and Chief Logan (15-2). The only loss was to Bishop Guilfoyle (16-9).

District 6 Tournament wins: Huntingdon (10-2); Marion Center (6-0); and Curwensville (2-1).

Bellefonte High School opened its baseball season on Tuesday, April 2, with a 2-1 victory over Lewistown at the Athletic Field.

Bob O'Leary singled to ignite the Raider two-run rally in the third. A sacrifice by Herb Beezer and a two-base error on Dan Leitzell's drive to center field made it 1-0. Tom Purnell, the Tribe starter, helped his own cause by singling home Leitzell for a 2-0 advantage.

The Panthers got on the board in the sixth on two walks and a two-out single.

Purnell retired the first nine men in order. He went six innings, yielded three hits, one run, walked two, and struck out five. Jeff Watson pitched the final frame and did not allow a hit. He walked one and struck out one.

On Wednesday, April 3, Jeff Watson got the start against Bishop Guilfoyle at the Athletic Field; but was greeted rudely by the visiting Marauders. After giving up three runs, one hit, and two walks, he was relieved by Dick Armstrong with two outs; but the Catholics continued their offense and had a 7-0 lead after two innings. In all, Coach Robinson used five pitchers including Denny Ebeling, Keith Haney, and Dan Leitzell in the 16-9 loss.

John Sommer hit a grand-slam for the Altoona boys in the 5th, and Denny DeWitt belted a 3-run homer for Bellefonte in the 4th. Watson (0-1) took the loss.

The Red Raiders upped their season's record to 2-1 with a 15-2 romp over Chief Logan at Yeagertown on Friday, April 5.

Bellefonte scored seven runs in the first inning and coasted to the victory. Tom Purnell slugged a pair of two-run homers and tripled home another tally. He was four for five in the contest.

Dan Leitzell went the first five innings, giving up five hits, two runs, one walk, and striking out thirteen Mingoes.

Jeff Watson pitched the last two innings, allowing only two hits, no runs, one walk, and struck out two.

The Tribe banged out a total of twelve hits off three Chief Logan pitchers.

At right: Pitcher Dan Leitzell

On Tuesday, April 16, the defending Central Penn League Champions indicated they had every intention of repeating, as they hammered Lock Haven, 27-1 in the league opener at the Bellefonte Athletic Field.

The Tribe pounded out 18 hits as senior Tom Purnell lead the assault with two doubles and two triples, six RBI's, and four runs scored. Denny DeWitt drove in four, while Sam Nastase, Frank Menna and Mel Harter drove in two apiece to give starting pitcher Dan Leitzell plenty of breathing room.

The Raiders wasted no time, jumping on Lou Christopher, the first of four Bobcat pitchers, for six runs in the first inning. Leadoff hitter Herb Beezer beat out a bunt and Menna followed suit. DeWitt singled home Beezer and Purnell doubled in Menna and DeWitt. Nastase singled and Harter tripled, and two more runs were on the board. Jim Probst relieved Christopher, but the Raiders weren't finished. Leitzell reached first on an error and Harter scored on the play. Probst got the final out on a strikeout, as the Tribe batted around.

Bellefonte broke the game wide open in the second, putting 15 more runs on the board. Menna led off with a walk, and then DeWitt tripled, scoring Menna. Purnell doubled in DeWitt and scored on consecutive singles by Nastase and Bruce Baney. Following walks to Bob O'Leary, Leitzell, and DeWitt, Purnell smashed a triple, plating three more Raiders. Two more singles, a walk, a stolen base, and a balk by Bob Brungard accounted for the rest of the runs as the Tribe batted around twice in the inning.

In the fourth, Coach Don Robinson began clearing his bench, as Bellefonte added four more runs on a Beezer triple and a two-run homer by DeWitt.

The Raiders finished scoring in the fifth, adding two more runs on two Lock Haven errors.

Leitzell picked up his first CPL win in a dominating performance. He yielded only two hits, three walks, and struck out five in his four innings of work. Jeff Watson pitched the final three innings, giving up one run, four hits, and striking out a pair of Bobcats.

Coach Don Robinson's Raiders pounded out 18 hits en route to a 27-1 victory over Lock Haven at the Athletic Field in Bellefonte. Winning pitcher Dan Leitzell was supported by Tom Purnell with 2 doubles, 2 triples, 6 RBI's, and 4 runs scored. Denny Dewitt drove in 4 with a home run and a double, while Sam Nastase, Frank Menna, and Mel Harter drove in 2 apiece.

Robby warned his Tribe that when they go to Lock Haven for a rematch, it wouldn't be that easy. His words proved to be prophetic, as the Bobcat's Ron Kodish, a southpaw and outstanding athlete, yielded only one run in a 1-0 Bellefonte win.

The Bellefonte Lumber Company continued its work on Friday, April 19, pounding out 12 hits in a 13-1 thumping of Penns Valley. The Raiders scored in every inning but the third off three pitchers used by Coach Ed Drapcho. Starter Jan Millon (0-1) took the loss.

The Tribe scored two in the first on a one-out single by Denny DeWitt, a stolen base, and Dan Leitzell's hit. Leitzell took second on the throw, moved to third on a wild pitch, and scored on a delayed steal with Fuss Nastase at first.

In the 2nd, two errors, a wild pitch, and Bob O'Leary's infield out made it 4-0.

Two walks, a wild pitch, a stolen base, and Herb Beezer's two-run single upped the lead to 6-0 in the fourth.

Gregg Wert replaced Millon to start the fifth and Leitzell greeted him with a single. Purnell followed with a home run. Purnell singled home two more runs in the sixth; and Bill Bierly's RBI single and a wild pitch accounted for Bellefonte's final runs in the seventh.

Purnell (1-0) was dominant on the mound, allowing one run on two hits, one walk, and striking out eleven in his seven innings.

Millon spoiled Purnell's bid for a shutout when he homered to right center with two down in the fourth. Robin Stover had a two-out single in the sixth for the other Ram hit.

On Tuesday, April 23, the Red Raiders rode into sole possession of first place in the Central Penn League on the arm of Dan Leitzell and the bat of Tom Purnell in a 3-2 victory over the Little Lions at Community Field in State College.

State College pushed across a run in the first inning on singles by Fred Watkins, Max Reese, and John Curley. Denny DeWitt made a great over-the-shoulder catch of Chuck Fedon's fly ball to deep center, limiting the Lions to a single tally.

In the third, Herb Beezer led off with a single, but was thrown out at the plate after Bill Bierly's single on a Fedon-to-Curley relay. Bellefonte tied the score when Purnell drove in Bierly, who had two hits on the day.

State went up 2-1 in the bottom of the third on a walk to Watkins, another Reese hit, and a squeeze bunt by Steve Blazer.

The Tribe came right back in the fourth and tied the game when Jerry Luckovich hit a liner to right which eluded Fedon and Luckovich circled the bases.

Bellefonte made it 3-2 in the seventh inning when Curley couldn't handle Frank Menna's towering pop-up behind home plate. Menna made the most of his new life by lining a double to right. DeWitt flied out to left for the second out; but Purnell poked his third single by Reese at short for a 3-2 lead.

Leitzell (2-0) shut down the Lions in the home half of the seventh and finished a great day with eleven strikeouts while yielding five hits and two walks.

The Tribe touched up Webb Moriarta for 10 hits. He walked 2, struck out 4.

Bellefonte, seeking its third consecutive Central Penn League Title, defeated Philipsburg, 1-0, on Monday, April 29, at the Athletic Field, improving its league record to 4-0.

Tom Purnell tossed a three-hitter, struck out 10, and walked two en route to his second victory. John Tekely (1-1) took the loss.

The Tribe threatened in the second, third, and fourth innings, stranding a total of seven men. Denny DeWitt was the only Raider with two hits on the day.

The Mounties of Gerry Davis had only a couple of scoring chances. In the sixth, the leadoff hitter singled, but Gary Yoder bunted into a double play on a fine play from Purnell to first baseman Bob O'Leary. A one-out single by Barry Abbott (his second single) in the seventh and a hit batsman put runners on first and second. However, Pete Prohaska grounded to third, and Purnell struck out the next batter and a pinch-hitter, ending the threat.

That set the stage for some Raider heroics in the bottom of the seventh. Leadoff batter O'Leary hit Tekely's first pitch to left center for a triple. Herb Beezer walked and stole second. Coach Don Robinson called for the suicide squeeze with left-hamd hitter Denny DeWitt at the plate. Tekely threw the pitch high and inside as O'Leary dashed for home; but DeWitt was able to bunt it foul. DeWitt eventually was retired on a grounder for the first out. Coach Davis called for an intentional walk to Dan Leitzell, loading the bases.

Purnell hit a shot to Greg Stine at third, who stopped it on a dive to his left, then threw home. It appeared that O'Leary was dead on arrival; but Umpire Jake Salsgiver ruled that Mountie catcher George Coval had dropped the ball on the collision at the plate and O'Leary was safe. Needless to say, O'Leary was mobbed by the Bellefonte bench after scoring the winning run.

Bellefonte avenged one of the losses to Bald Eagle last season by clipping the Eagles at Unionville on Tuesday, April 30. Dan Leitzell (3-0) struck out eight and pitched out of a couple of jams of his own making in the 5-0 victory.

The Raiders threatened in the first with one out, advancing men to second and third; but John Simpson (1-2), the losing pitcher, got a grounder and strikeout to halt the threat.

The Tribe scored in the third as Herb Beezer singled, advanced to second on a fielder's choice, and came home on Denny DeWitt's single to center. DeWitt was thrown out at second trying to stretch the hit into a double.

In the bottom of the 3rd, Leitzell walked the first two men; and then uncorked a wild pitch, moving them up. He then bore down, striking out the next two hitters; and a great defensive play by third baseman Sam Nastase prevented any damage.

Bellefonte boosted its lead in the fifth to 3-0. Bill Bierly's one-out single and steal of second put him in position to score on Tom Purnell's double.

Nastase singled home Purnell; but was thrown out trying to take second on the throw to the plate.

A Bierly free pass and DeWitt's two-run homer ended the scoring for the Tribe. Bierly and DeWitt had half of the Red Raider's 10 hits off Simpson.

Bald Eagle threatened again in the bottom of the seventh. Larry Wiser led off with a single; and after pinch-hitter Bill Dorman had struck out, Dave Etters, another pinch-hitter, drew a walk as did the next batter Simpson. With the bases loaded, Gary Bartley lined to Jerry Luckovich in right field, who relayed the ball back to first to nip Simpson for a game-ending double play.

The Raiders had a big game coming up with Bald Eagle Area on the road. Sam "Fuss" Nastase was getting off the bus and he stopped to ask Robby why he was batting Dan Leitzell at the lower end of the order. Robby replied, "I'll tell you after the game is over." Leitzell was Bellefonte's top pitcher; and an excellent hitter with power. More than anything, Robby needed his ace to focus totally on pitching that day. The Eagles had a good team loaded with very good hitters and Leitzell was able to shut them down. When the Raiders got back to their locker room in Bellefonte, Nastase walked by Robby and said, "Good choice today."

On Tuesday, May 7, Bellefonte demonstrated its power at the plate as Denny DeWitt and Mel Harter doubled; and DeWitt, Sam Nastase, and Tom Purnell hit home runs. In all, the Tribe pounded out 10 hits in a 10-5 victory over Penns Valley at the Athletic Field, as they moved one step closer to another league pennant. Bill Bierly, Harter, Purnell, and DeWitt each had two hits for Bellefonte.

The Rams never recovered from Nastase's three-run homer in the first inning, and trailed by 9-0 in the fourth when Purnell hit a two-run homer. DeWitt's shot in the sixth ended the scoring for Bellefonte.

Doug Stover drove in one run for the visitors in the fifth; and another scored on a wild pitch. The Rams added three more in the seventh, one on a wild pitch and the other two on Steve Walker's single. Jan Millon had three hits to pace the Penns Valley attack; and Bob Snyder added a pair.

Dan Leitzell (4-0) went four innings, allowed three hits, no runs, no walks, and struck out seven. Denny Ebeling pitched the fifth and sixth; and Keith Haney and Purnell combined to complete the seventh.

Fred Price (0-1) took the loss. He was relieved by Weyman in the fifth with two outs.

Lock Haven was the scene of a classic pitching duel between Tom Purnell of the Red Raiders and Ron Kodish of the Bobcats on Wednesday, May 8, as Bellefonte came away with a 1-0 victory.

Purnell gave up only one hit, a fourth inning double by catcher Jeff Knarr. He struck out seven to up his record to 3-0. Only three balls were hit out of the infield—a fly to Denny DeWitt in center, another fly to Mel Harter in right, and Knarr's double to left. Purnell has now pitched three complete games and has given up only one run.

Kodish (1-1) was also impressive, limiting the high-powered Raider offence to five hits, one walk, and striking out 10.

Bellefonte put a run on the board in the fourth when Dan Leitzell led off with a walk, stole second, and went to third on a wild pitch. Kodish fanned the next two hitters; and got two quick strikes on Bruce Baney before the Raider catcher banged a single up the middle, scoring Leitzell.

Lock Haven threatened in its half of the fourth. Knarr doubled and Kodish walked with two outs. Baney then threw out Knarr attempting to steal third.

The Tribe mounted only one other threat. In the sixth, Leitzell drilled a one-out double down the right field line, but was thrown out attempting a steal of third.

Baney and Leitzell each had two hits for the Raiders.

On Friday, May 10, at the Athletic Field in Bellefonte, the Raiders of Coach Don Robinson clinched a tie for the league title by beating State College, 6-3.

The visitors drew first blood by scoring three runs early in the contest. Rod Owens tripled and scored on an error for a 1-0 lead. Infield hits by Webb Moriarta, Dwight Knode, Chuck Fedon, and Bruce Blaser accounted for two more tallies.

Bellefonte scored twice in the fourth on a Denny DeWitt single and a two-run home run by pitcher Dan Leitzell.

In the sixth, the Tribe went on top, 6-3, as losing Lion pitcher Knode (1-1) gave up singles to Tom Purnell and Sam Nastase. Following two State College errors, Coach Bob Smith brought in Max Reese; and Bruce Baney hit his first pitch for a triple. Baney was brought home on a Bill Bierly single.

Knode was responsible for five runs, eight hits, and one walk. Reese gave up three hits and one run in one-third of an inning. Crouse mopped up, recording nothing but zeros. The State College pitching corps did not strike out a single Red Raider.

Leitzell (5-0), went the full seven innings, allowing seven hits, three runs, two walks, and striking out five.

On Tuesday, May 14, the Red Raiders of Coach Don Robinson won their third consecutive Central Penn League Title and fourth in five years since he has been at the helm in Bellefonte.

The Tribe had to come from behind twice to tie the score; and in the seventh inning, scored four runs for a 6-2 victory at Philipsburg.

The pitching duel between Bellefonte's Tom Purnell and Philipsburg's John Tekely never materialized, as the Mounties collected eight hits and two runs off Purnell; and the Raiders pounded out 12 hits and 6 runs off Tekely and reliever Frank Peulla.

Dan Leitzell took over in the fifth inning and closed the door on the Mounties. He allowed only one hit the rest of the way in picking up his sixth win.

Philipsburg scored first in the bottom of the third. Harry Socie lined a one-out single, went to second on Gary Yoder's bunt single and scored on a Don Stine liner off Purnell's leg into right center.

Bellefonte tied the game in the 4th when Purnell singled and advanced to second on a bobble by the center fielder. He scored on a single to right by Sam Nastase.

Down 2-1 in the 6th, the Raider's Purnell reached first on a fielder's choice, moved to third on a Nastase single, and scored on a single by Bruce Baney.

Bellefonte exploded for four runs in the seventh. A leadoff single by Bob O'Leary, a walk to Denny DeWitt, an error, and consecutive singles by Purnell, Nastase, Baney, and Bill Bierly gave the Raiders the championship.

Bellefonte put the lid on a perfect 10-0 season in the CPL with a 4-3 win over Bald Eagle Area on Friday, May 17, at the Athletic Field.

The Raiders overcame a 3-0 deficit and scored the winning run with two outs in the bottom of the seventh.

BEA pushed across two runs in the second. Denny Kolasa led off with a single, advanced to second on a Larry Wiser bunt, and scored on Steve Wiser's single up the middle. Steve Wiser moved to second on the throw home, advanced to third on a passed ball, and scored on a dropped pop-up in short center.

The Eagles made it 3-0 in the fifth when Curt Heverly lashed a one-out triple down the right field line and scored on an infield error.

In the bottom of the fifth, a single by Jerry Luckovich, two errors, and fielder's choices on grounders by Denny DeWitt and Dan Leitzell loaded the bases with two out. Tom Purnell's single to center scored two, and Sam Nastase singled in the tying run before losing pitcher John Simpson (3-4) got a strikeout.

In the seventh, DeWitt reached first on an error at short, went to second when the center fielder misplayed the ball, advanced to third on Purnell's fly to deep center, and scored when Nastase's grounder was booted at third.

Purnell (4-0) went 7 innings, allowed 4 hits, 3 runs, one walk, and struck out 5.

At the annual Central Penn Scholastic Baseball League meeting held at the Bellefonte Elks Club on Wednesday May 22, Bellefonte Athletic Director John Miller accepted the championship trophy on behalf of Coach Don Robinson, who was not present due to an illness in his family.

A proposed rule change would allow the head coach and one of his assistants to coach from the baselines. The present rule requires that the coaching boxes be occupied by players. In addition, plans were formulated to select an all-star team for the 1969 season.

On Tuesday, June 2, after a long layoff, Bellefonte High School cleared the first hurdle in its quest for a District 6 title by defeating Huntingdon, 10-2, at Community Field in State College.

Dan Leitzell's bat and Tom Purnell's arm carried the Raiders to another come-from-behind victory. In all, the Raiders pounded out 10 hits.

The Bearcats went on top, 2-0, in the first inning on two errors, two walks, and another error.

In the third, the Tribe came storming back. Bob O'Leary was hit by a pitch, and walks to Denny DeWitt and Herb Beezer loaded the bases. Leitzell hit a grand-slam homer down the left field line for a 4-2 Bellefonte lead.

The Raiders added four more runs in the top of the fifth. Leitzell opened with a walk, and Purnell doubled him home. Purnell moved to third when Sam Nastase's grounder was booted by Jim Black at second. A delayed steal enabled Purnell to score and Nastase to move to third. Bruce Baney got aboard on a fielder's choice and Mel Harter singled to left, driving in Nastase. Baney was thrown out trying to reach third. Harter then stole second and came home on a single by O'Leary.

Bellefonte scored its final two runs in the sixth on three walks, three stolen bases, a balk, and two passed balls.

Starting pitcher Leitzell had control problems in his one and two-thirds innings, and allowed two runs while walking four.

Purnell (6-0 overall), yielded only one hit in four and a third innings, walked two, and struck out six.

Denny Ebeling mopped up, walking one and striking out 2 in one inning pitched.

At right: Mel Harter

On Thursday, June 6, Bellefonte (14-1), qualified for the District 6 title game at Penn State's Beaver Field by blanking Marion Center (11-4) in a semi-final game at Altoona, 6-0.

Dan Leitzell (8-0 overall) pitched a 5-hit shutout; and Coach Don Robinson's Raiders took advantage of 9 Stinger errors and some timely hitting by Bill Bierly, the only two-hit man in the Bellefonte lineup.

Marion Center loaded the bases in the first on a walk and two singles; but Leitzell bore down, striking out the next two batters, and nailing Terry Roof in his attempt to steal home.

In the fourth frame, Bellefonte made it 3-0 on a two-out single by Bruce Baney, a bad-hop double by Bierly, two errors, a stolen base, a single by Jerry Luckovich, and a wild pitch. The Raiders had seven hits off two Stinger pitchers.

Marion Center threatened in the final inning; but after a Paul Lingenfelter double, a fine relay from the outfield to home recorded the third out.

Marion Center Coach Ted Holtz and Bellefonte Assistant Coach Ralph Gray were teammates on the Barnesboro American Legion baseball team. They both graduated from Indiana State College.

In the 1968 playoff game against Marion Center with Dan Leitzell on the mound and a 10-0 advantage, Robby make some substitutions. One of them was Don Lucas, the backup second baseman. On the way home in the bus, Lucas shook his hand and thanked him for getting into the game. Lucas was with the Bellefonte program for four years. He became a successful softball coach at Penns Valley High School, winning a State Championship. His teams reflected the kind of player he was—a hustler with a great attitude; and someone who would do anything you asked.

On June 7, Bellefonte (15-1) won the District 6 Championship with a 2-1 victory over Gary Orwig's Curwensville Golden Tide (8-4) at Penn State's Beaver Field in State College. Tom Purnell struck out 13 and got the win, while Ron Stewart, who went on to play at Arizona State, took the loss.

Gary Orwig was a Centre Hall product and former Bellefonte resident.

Bellefonte's Denny Dewitt had 2 hits including a double and scored the winning run on a passed ball. He also threw out Harry Rogers at home plate late in the game, cutting off the potential tying run. Both boys later played the outfield for Penn State and became good friends.

Coach Don Robinson's Raiders had several opportunities to break the game open, but could not come up with a clutch hit.

Curwensville High, whose colors are black and gold, was taking batting practice when the Bellefonte bus arrived at Penn State's Beaver Field on Friday, June 7. Coach Don Robinson remarked, "It looks like we're playing the Pittsburgh Pirates."

The Golden Tide scored their lone run in the first. With two out, Rogers bounced a single over Purnell's glove and scored moments later when Stewart doubled into the gap in right center.

Bellefonte stranded a runner at third in the bottom half of the first.

In the second inning, the Tribe tied the score when Sam Nastase led off with a single to left. An error on Bruce Baney's grounder put runners on first and third. One out later, Mel Harter was hit by a pitch; and on Bob O'Leary's infield out, Nastase scored, Baney moved to third, and Harter to second. A strikeout stranded the pair of runners.

DeWitt drilled a double to center to lead off the third inning. After stealing third, he scored on a passed ball. Nastase and Baney had been issued free passes in the inning, but died at second and third.

In the sixth, Harry Rogers singled and promptly stole second. Ron Stewart, the losing pitcher, struck out for the second time. However, Jim Bailor singled to center, and speed demon Rogers dashed for the plate. DeWitt uncorked a perfect throw to catcher Bruce Baney who held onto the ball in tagging out Rogers. Coach

Orwig argued the call to no avail.

Tom Purnell (7-0 overall) struck out the side in the seventh. On the day, he allowed seven hits, one run, walked one, and struck out 13.

Stewart yielded four hits, two runs, three walks, and struck out 7.

At left: Jubilant Raiders hoist Coach Robinson on their shoulders, celebrating their first District 6 title.

Dan Leitzell (8-0)   **Tom Purnell (7-0)**

Dan Leitzell and Tom Purnell were Coach Don Robinson's 1-2 punch in the 1968 season. When one of them pitched, the other played shortstop; and they were both very productive at the plate and efficient in the field. Leitzell had a great curve to go along with his fast ball; and Purnell had a nasty knuckleball to go along with his heater.

Owen Dougherty, the baseball coach at Indiana State College, attended the District 6 Championship game between Bellefonte and Curwensville. He was interested in Tom Purnell.

Dougherty, a former Penn Stater, was Ralph Gray's backfield coach at Indiana State College.

The 1968 Bellefonte Junior Varsity Season

The 25-man roster included the following youngsters: Denny Young, Alan Leitzell, Dan Faulkner, Bob Emel, Fred Johnson, Joe Quici, Grant Torsell, Bill Luther, Dick Armstrong, Glenn Leiter, Tom Frantz, Dan Anderson, Bob Davidson, Harry Hunt, Greg Brown, Duane Kline, and Bob Sheaffer.

Coach Ralph Gray's junior varsity only lost one game—that being an abbreviated contest at Millheim. The Penns Valley Rams defeated the Raiders 6-5 in a contest that ended at 6 p.m. due to a school-imposed curfew.

Pitchers Dick Armstrong and Dan Faulkner were very effective, not losing a single game.

Wins: Lock Haven (5-2); Penns Valley (17-4); Philipsburg (5-2 & 5-3); State College (6-2); and Bald Eagle Area (4-2 & 5-1).

World Series: Detroit Tigers over the St. Louis Cardinals, 4-3.

College World Series Champion: USC.

Little League World Series Champion: Wakayama, Osaka, Japan.

1969 Bellefonte High School Varsity Baseball Team
First Row, L-R: Glenn Leiter, Denny Ebeling, Don Lucas, Fred Johnson, Keith Haney, Dave O'Shell, Joe Quici. **Row 2:** Coach Don Robinson, Jeff Watson, Denny Dewitt, Bob Shaffer, Albert Leitzell, Jimmy Grey, Tom Knoffsinger, Bill Luther, Frank Nolan, Manager Greg Rishel. **Row 3:** Bob Emel, Dan Faulkner, Frank Oesterling, Sam Nastase, Jim Bell, Dick Armstrong, Manager Bob Wallace.

The Red Raiders were 6-4 in the Central Penn League. Wins: Bald Eagle Area (4-2 & 13-2); Philipsburg (7-4); State College (2-1); and Penns Valley (11-4 & 14-8). Losses: Philipsburg (4-3); State College (5-3); and Lock Haven (7-4 & 3-2).

Four more wins made the Bellefonte overall record 10-4: Lewistown (5-3); Juniata (6-5 & 15-4); and Chief Logan (6-3).

On May 12, Bellefonte defeated Penns Valley, 14-8. Robby's Raiders scored 10 runs in the 3rd inning to breeze to their sixth win in ten outings. Fred Johnson, Dave O'Shell, and Denny DeWitt led the way to victory. In the big inning, DeWitt hit a 3-run homer to right. Dick Armstrong picked up the win.

1969 Action at the Athletic Field in Bellefonte

Bellefonte High School's Athletic Director "Big John" Miller had a definition of the word *uniform* that was his own—not changing in form or character, remaining the same in all cases and at all times.

For at least 17 years, the Red Raiders had the same uniform—a gray wool jersey with a maroon "B" on the left chest and a maroon hat with a white "B." Each year Miller would add a few of those uniforms to the high school baseball wardrobe.

It wasn't until 1968, after Robby's Raiders had won four Central Penn League Titles and a District 6 Championship in five years, that Coach Robinson was able to order new uniforms; so the 1969 baseball team donned a different style of uniform—gray with red trim, and a red hat with a white "B."

From then on, the varsity uniforms were passed down to the junior varsity team, so Coach Gray always had 20 uniforms. At the end of spring tryouts, he would hand out 18 and hold two of them back. He encouraged those boys who didn't get a uniform to come to practice the following week and try to earn one. In all of his years of coaching, only one boy, Neil Shaw, ever did that; and he got a uniform.

Coach Don Robinson

Bellefonte bench at the Athletic Field

1969 Bellefonte High School Junior Varsity Baseball Team

First Row, L-R: Ed Runkle, Denny Gibbons, Roger McKinley, Bob Davidson, Terry Cable, Homer Hosterman, Manager Jim Schreffler. **Row 2:** Elwood Crater, Barry Bitner, Doug Hazel, Bob Luther, Rodney McCulley, Bill Hoy, Denny Hile, Joe Conaway, Manager Rick Cartwright. **Row 3:** Ladden Krebs, Dan Anderson, Doug Leathers, Gary Rockey, Don Hazel, George Kline, Frank Kelley, Mike Swartz, Coach Ralph Gray.

When Robinson and Gray began coaching in 1964, the Central Penn League did not permit coaches to be in the coaching boxes at first and third bases.
It was referred to as "The Gerry Davis Rule."

Robby gives instructions to the Bellefonte runner at third base.

1970 Bellefonte High School Varsity Baseball Team

First Row, L-R: Bob Wallace, Dan Stevens, Bob Davidson, Tom Frantz, Bucky Quici, Tom Rhoads, Dave Williams, Manager Cliff Hodgson. **Row 2:** Denny Hile, Dick Armstrong, Glenn Leiter, Dave O'Shell, Al Leitzell, Fred Johnson, Grant Torsell, Coach Don Robinson. **Row 3:** Bill Hoy, Dan Faulkner, Jon Kerschner, Bill Luther, Bob Luther, Frank Nolan, Doug Sassman.

The 1970 Red Raiders were 6-4 in the Central Penn League and 7-6 overall. CPL Wins: Lock Haven (16-3 & 7-3); Philipsburg (6-1 & 3-2); Penns Valley (20-5); State College (3-2). League losses: Bald Eagle (2-1 & 5-2); Penns Valley (3-2); State College (4-2).

In other games, Bellefonte defeated Chief Logan, 10-9; and lost to Lewistown, 8-2, as well as Juniata, 4-2.

1970 Bellefonte High School Junior Varsity Team
First Row, L-R: Tom Eckley, Dan Shuey, Dave Gehret, John Zeleznick, Bat Boy Billy Gray.
Row 2: Jeff Webster, Tim Thompson, Bill Kovacic, Kim Haney, Al Crafts, Pat Kelly. **Row 3:**
John Eckley, Frank Kelley, Gary Drapcho, Larry Saylor, Steve Crowley, Leonard Young, Steve
Gibboney, Coach Ralph Gray.

April 22—Tom Seaver struck out 19 San Diego Padres in a 2-1 Mets win.

June 12—Doc Ellis of the Pittsburgh Pirates pitched a no-hitter against the San
Diego Padres in a 2-0 Pirate win.

July 16—Pittsburgh's Three Rivers Stadium opened to the public. The Cincinnati
Reds beat the Pirates 4-3.

World Series: The Baltimore Orioles beat the Cincinnati Reds, 4-1.

College World Series Champion: University of Southern California.

Little League World Series Champion: Wayne, New Jersey.

Pittsburgh Pirates won the Eastern Division with an 89-73 record.

1971

Key losses from the 1970 Bellefonte High School Varsity Baseball Team, which went 6-4 in the Central Penn League: Fred Johnson, Dave O'Shell, Glenn Leiter, Bucky Quici, Bill Luther, and Dick Armstrong.

Six lettermen returned for the 1971 season: Tom Rhoads, Denny Hile, Al Leitzell, Doug Sassman, Bob Davidson, and Bill Hoy.

Varsity reserves: Homer Hosterman, Terry Cable, Ray McClure, Greg Tressler, Yogi Leitzell, Jim Bell, Skip Reichert, Mike Watson, Steve Dalena, Doug Leathers, Mike Rhoads, Gary Drapcho, and Frank "Machine Gun" Kelley.

Coach Don Robinson and Assistant Coach Denny Leathers began practice with a total of 35 candidates.

The Bellefonte Teachers went on strike on Monday, May 10. At that time, the Raiders were 5-2 in the Central Penn League and 6-3 overall. The game with Bald Eagle Area on May 10 had to be forfeited, along with remaining games with Philipsburg and Penns Valley. Final CPL record: 5-5. Overall: 6-6.

Wins: Penns Valley (7-1* & 10-0); State College (5-3 & 5-3); and Lock Haven (2-1 & 5-2). Losses: Altoona (12-3); Bald Eagle (4-3); and Philipsburg (6-2).

Forfeit losses: Bald Eagle (7-0); Philipsburg (7-0); Penns Valley (7-0).

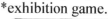

*exhibition game.

Bill Hoy   **Yogi Leitzell**   **Mike Watson**

On Thursday, April 8, Yogi Leitzell's grand slam home run in the 4th inning accounted for most of the runs in the 7-1 exhibition win over Penns Valley. Leitzell and Doug Leathers collected two hits apiece as right-hander Bill Hoy earned the victory for the Red Raiders.

Bellefonte pitcher Bill Hoy picked off a Little Lion at second base in the fourth inning; and another at first base in the seventh inning and stymied the State College offense in a 5-3 victory on Tuesday, April 13. Al Leitzell had two hits including a grand-slam homer and Tom Rhoads added a pair of singles.

On Friday, April 16, Bob Davidson scattered six Lock Haven hits, walked one, and struck out 11 in a 2-1 Bellefonte victory. The Raiders played errorless baseball in the field.

After being sidelined for two weeks, Bellefonte's Bill Hoy came back with a dazzling performance in a 5-3 win over State College on Friday, April 30, on the road. He spotted the Lions a 2-0 lead in the first inning; but with one out in the second, he retired 13 straight batters and bore down in the late innings when State threatened to tie the game. Second baseman Bob Davidson had a good day at the plate for the Raiders.

In 1971, the Bellefonte Junior Varsity team began practicing and playing games at the Teener Field in Parkview Heights. Previously, a make-shift field at the Bellefonte Middle School was utilized.

Junior Varsity Coach Ralph Gray welcomed 25 candidates for 1971. Those that saw action in the abbreviated schedule were: Al Crafts, Dave Gehret, Dan Shuey, Larry Saylor, Todd Cable, John Eckley, Lenny Young, Steve Crowley, Gary Drapcho, Keith Haney, Bill Kovacic, Jeff Webster, Joe Williams, Paul McCaslin, John Zeleznick, Pat Kelly, Tim Thompson, and Tom Eckley.

The team had a 6-2 record for the season. Wins: Penns Valley (15-3 & 12-5); State College (9-5); Lock Haven (11-4 & 11-10); and Philipsburg (11-2). Losses: State College (5-3) and Bald Eagle Area (10-7).

1972 Bellefonte High School Varsity Baseball Team
Central Penn League Champions

First Row, L-R: Mike Rhoads, Chuck Riglin, Steve Dalena, Ken Grubb. **Row 2:** Terry Cable, Harold Reichert, Alan Crafts, Dave Gehret, Doug Sassman, Jerry Leitzell, Todd Cable, Ray McClure. **Row 3:** Coach Don Robinson, Tom Burger, Larry Saylor, Doug Hazel, Lenny Young, Frank Kelley, Doug Leathers, Pat Kelly, Mike Watson, Assistant Coach Denny Leathers.

The 1972 Red Raiders finished the regular season with a 12-0 record in the Central Penn League and 13-2 overall. They were victorious over Penns Valley (10-1 & 19-2); Clearfield (7-0 & 12-4); Bald Eagle Area (10-2 & 7-1); Philipsburg-Osceola (11-4 & 2-1); Lock Haven (7-1 & 15-1); and State College (10-1 & 10-0). In exhibition play, Bellefonte beat Tyrone, 4-3 and lost to Altoona, 8-4. In the District VI Playoffs, the Raiders lost to Curwensville, 5-3.

Bellefonte shortstop Todd Cable led the Central Penn League in hitting.

Robby was about to pitch batting practice, so he gave his keys to the high school locker room to Manager Mike Sprankle to hold. Shortly after, Mike was looking for lost balls in the field along the first base line. When Robby finally asked for the keys, Sprankle said "I think I lost them". Sprankle and the rest of the baseball team accompanied Robby onto the field where they proceeded to look for the keys. They found some baseballs, but not the keys. One of the players asked Robby what was hanging around his neck; and it turned out the missing set of keys was inside his shirt. Seems that Sprankle forgot he gave them back to Robby, and Robby forgot that they had been returned to him.

Graduation took the heart of Coach Don Robinson's pitching corps, Bill Hoy and Bob Davidson. Additional key losses were: Al Leitzell, Denny Hile, Gregg Tressler, and Tom Rhoads.

Back from the 1971 squad that finished 5-5 in the Central Penn League: Mike Watson, Doug Leathers, Terry Cable, Jerry "Yogi" Leitzell, and Doug Sassman.

Pitching candidates included: Tom Burger, Gary Drapcho, Steve Dalena, Frank Kelley, and Ray McClure. The remaining candidates: Dave Gehret, Todd Cable, Mike Rhoads, Lenny Young, Larry Saylor, Kenny Grubb, Chuck Riglin, Al Crafts, Skip Reichert, and Pat Kelly.

Robinson will be assisted by Denny Leathers, while Ralph Gray will handle the Junior Varsity squad.

Clearfield joined the Central Penn League effective for the 1972 season.

The Red Raiders opened the 1972 season with a 4-3 win over Tyrone at the Athletic Field in Bellefonte on Thursday, April 6.

The Tribe scored three times in the third inning on a one-out single by winning pitcher Tom Burger, a single by Doug Sassman, a walk to Al Crafts, a bases-loaded walk to Yogi Leitzell, and Mike Watson's two-run single.

In the top of the sixth, Mike Stever sparked a three-run Tyrone uprising with a two-run single.

The 3-3 tie was broken in the bottom of the sixth on walks to Watson, Larry Saylor, Todd Cable, and Dave Gehret by Tyrone pitchers Harris and Leasure.

Tom Burger went seven innings, allowed three runs on three hits, two walks, while striking out nine.

On Tuesday, April 11, the Raiders exploded for nine runs in the first inning at the Athletic Field in Bellefonte, and coasted to a 10-1 victory over Penns Valley.

A single by Doug Sassman, an error, and five walks chased lefty Ram starter Brian Miller; and with one out in the opening frame Coach Jeff Wert had to call on reliever Ed Furner. Another error allowed Tom Burger to reach base; and a Doug Leathers single followed by a three-run homer by Yogi Leitzell gave Bellefonte a 9-0 advantage.

The Penns Valley pitching corps allowed a total of ten walks and six hits. Leathers and Terry Cable each had a pair of singles.

Three Raider pitchers—Tom Burger, Gary Drapcho, and Steve Dalena combined for 13 strikeouts, 3 walks, and allowed only one Ram hit, that being a single by Tom Garman. Burger worked the first three innings and got the win.

Coach Don Robinson still had to find a second pitcher to go along with Tom Burger, who was the number one stopper for the Tribe.

Jeff Wert succeeded Ed Drapcho and coached the Rams for five years.

Bellefonte travelled to Driving Park in Clearfield on Friday, April 14, and defeated the league newcomer, 7-0, for its second win.

For the first three innings, Raider pitcher Tom Burger and Bison ace Ken Stewart were locked up in a mound duel, and put zeros on the board.

Clearfield threatened in the first with one out when Steve Harper doubled and Jerry Bickle singled. However, a perfect relay got Harper in a rundown for the second out, and Burger struck out Clayt Ireland to end the inning. Harper and Bickle were the only 2-hit men in the game.

The Tribe had a 5-run uprising in the fourth. With one out, Doug Hazel reached base on the first of four Clearfield errors in the inning. One out later, Todd Cable drew a walk, and brother Terry drilled a 3-2 pitch inside the bag at third for a double, scoring Hazel and putting Todd on third. Burger hit a popup behind second which popped out of the second baseman's glove, allowing two runs to score. Consecutive errors on grounders by Doug Sassman and Yogi Leitzell accounted for the final two runs of the inning.

Bellefonte tacked on two insurance runs in the sixth. Terry Cable got aboard on an error and a single by Sassman put runners on first and second. Another error loaded the bases and Doug Leathers plated two runs with a single.

In the Bison sixth, Harper and Bickle singled; but Burger fanned the next 3 batters. Burger struck out 8, walked 2, and yielded 6 hits for his second win.

Robby's Raiders got 5 hits, 4 walks, and played errorless baseball.

At the Athletic Field in Bellefonte on Tuesday, April 18, Altoona led 5-4 after five innings; and added two runs in the sixth and one in the seventh for an 8-4 win over the Raiders.

Dave Gehret had a 2-run pinch-hit double, and Larry Saylor's single drove in a pair. Todd Cable had the only other Raider hit.

Gary Drapcho absorbed the loss, going three innings, allowing four runs on four hits, six walks, and striking out two. Steve Dalena went two innings, yielding one run, two hits, one walk, and striking out two Mountain Lions. Tom Burger mopped up and relinquished three hits, three runs, two walks, while striking out three in his two innings of work.

On the bus headed for Unionville on Friday, April 21, Bellefonte Coach Don Robinson and his assistant Denny Leathers discussed who should play right field for the Raiders on that day against Bald Eagle Area. Mike Rhoads hit a couple of shots in batting practice, so he got the start and responded with four hits in four at-bats including a double, two stolen bases, and scored twice to spark the Tribe to a 10-2 victory. Yogi Leitzell had two hits for the Raiders.

The visitors jumped on Eagle starter and losing pitcher Dave Kresovich for a run in the first inning on a single by Yogi Leitzell, a fielder's choice by Doug Sassman, an infield out, and a single by Doug Hazel.

Bellefonte broke the game open in the fourth on singles by Rhoads, Terry Cable, Tom Burger, and Leitzell, three walks, and a Mike Watson sacrifice which put the Tribe up, 5-0.

A double by Rhoads and an error made it 6-0 in the sixth; and Bellefonte added two more runs in the seventh on singles by Todd Cable, Rhoads, Al Crafts, Ray McClure, and a walk to Terry Cable.

Raider pitcher Tom Burger had the lid on the Eagles until the fifth inning. Bob DeArment bounced a two-out single off Leitzell's chest at third. Although that was the only hit off Burger, the Eagles were hitting the ball hard, right at someone; and the Raider ace had issued five free passes while striking out six.

Still looking for a second pitcher, Robinson inserted Ray McClure in the sixth and the right-hander allowed two hits, two runs, walked two, and struck out four in his two innings pitched.

Coach Don Robinson's team, playing solid defense, getting tough pitching from Tom Burger and timely base hits from the lower half of the batting order, enabled them to overcome a 4-0 deficit at Philipsburg on Tuesday, April 25, and emerge victorious by an 11-4 count.

The Mounties of Coach Gerry Davis went on top, 2-0, in the first inning on a walk to Dave Lamb, singles by Greg Smeal and Barry Miller and walks to Lynn Gilham and Jim Wigfield.

Philipsburg added two more runs in the third aided by an error and singles by Smeal, Gary Volk, and Wigfield.

In the fourth frame, Bellefonte loaded the bases against losing pitcher Doug Hazelton on singles by Doug Sassman and Doug Leathers, and an error on Doug Hazel's fielder's choice. A walk to Mike Watson scored Sassman and Todd Cable's grounder forced Leathers at the plate; but Mike Rhoads' sacrifice fly scored Hazel, cutting the Mountie lead in half.

Winning pitcher Burger (5-0) led off the fifth with a line-drive double to left and moved to third on Yogi Leitzell's single. A walk to Sassman loaded the bases but Leathers lined out at second. A Hazel single plated Burger and an error on Watson's grounder allowed Leitzell to score the tying run. Another error permitted Sassman to score before Rhoads hit a clutch double off reliever Chuck Abbott putting Bellefonte in front, 8-4.

The Tribe added three more in the sixth on a walk to Sassman, a Leathers double, a sacrifice fly by Hazel, singles by the Cable brothers, and an error.

Burger went 7 innings, allowed 7 hits, 4 runs, 6 walks, and struck out 4.

The Raiders' rise to the top of the Central Penn League can be attributed to the kind of baseball a Robinson-coached team played—no costly mistakes, taking advantage of their opponents' mistakes, timely hitting, great defense, and strong pitching. His players developed confidence in themselves due to the fact that he let them know he had confidence in them.

In a game against Lock Haven at the Athletic Field in Bellefonte on Friday, April 28, Coach Don Robinson found what he has been looking for all season—a second starting pitcher. Ray McClure went the distance against the Bobcats, yielding only one run on five hits, one walk, while striking out eight for his first win and a 7-1 Raider victory.

The Tribe wasted no time getting on the board in the first inning on a solo home run by Doug Sassman and a single by Mike Watson, driving in Doug Hazel who had stroked a two-out triple.

Lock Haven scored in the fourth on a John Condo leadoff triple and an error on the relay. The Bobcats recorded two singles; but McClure pitched out of the jam.

Bellefonte took a 4-1 lead in the bottom of the fourth on three Lock Haven errors, a sacrifice bunt by Terry Cable, and singles by McClure and Yogi Leitzell.

The Raiders tacked on three insurance runs on a sacrifice fly by Leitzell and Sassman's two-run single to right field.

Hazel drilled a triple with one out in the fifth; but was stranded at third.

Five of Bellefonte's seven runs were scored by the last three men in the lineup—Mike Rhoads, Terry Cable, and McClure.

Sassman in the fifth and Todd Cable in the seventh contributed great defensive plays for the Tribe.

Bellefonte centerfielder Doug Sassman was also an outstanding wrestler. Last month he participated in an Old Timer's wrestling meet which raised a question about his remaining eligibility. The P.I.A.A. ruled the meet was not an All-Star contest, so the Raiders did not have to forfeit the games in which he had played after the meet. The good news arrived on Friday morning, May 5, the same day the Raiders were scheduled to play Penns Valley at Millheim; and proved to be bad news for the Rams, as Sassman went two for four, scored once, and drove in three runs in a 19-2 Bellefonte win.

The Tribe jumped on starter Gary Stine (1-2) for seven runs in the first on singles by Doug Leathers, Todd Cable, and Sassman plus walks to Mike Watson, Terry Cable, winning pitcher Tom Burger (6-0), and a pair of errors.

Bellefonte scored 8 more runs in the sixth sparked by a Larry Saylor double, singles by Yogi Leitzell and Watson, in addition to 6 walks and a Ram error.

Leathers, Doug Hazel, Watson, and Todd Cable had 8 of Bellefonte's 13 hits.

Bellefonte's game scheduled for May 2 with State College and its game scheduled for May 9 with Clearfield were both postponed; so there was some confusion in re whom the Raiders would be playing on Wednesday, May 10 at the Athletic Field in Bellefonte. A league rule determined that the State game must be played first, so the Clearfield game was re-scheduled for Thursday, May 11.

Ray McClure (2-0) went seven innings, allowed one run on four hits, walked one and struck out two in beating State College 10-1.

State went on top, 1-0 in the first when Steve Hackman bunted for a single, stole second, went to third on a Tom Fry single and scored on a sac fly to center by Jeff Smith.

Bellefonte jumped on starter Butch Tate (0-3) for three hits and four runs, sending 10 men to the plate in its half of the first. Yogi Leitzell led off with a single, moved to second when Doug Sassman walked, but was erased on Doug Leathers' fielder's choice. A Doug Hazel single plated Sassman and Leathers scored on the throw from the outfield. A walk to Mike Watson, a Todd Cable single, and a bases-loaded walk to Mike Rhoads accounted for two more runs.

The Tribe added three more runs in the fourth on singles by Sassman and Todd Cable, a pair of walks, a double steal, and a passed ball.

Bellefonte completed its scoring in the sixth on a Larry Saylor double, two Little Lion errors and another Todd Cable single.

Todd Cable had 3 of the Tribe's 10 hits; and Yogi Leitzell had a pair of singles.

Bellefonte and Clearfield combined for 23 hits and 16 runs on Thursday, May 11, at the Athletic Field in Bellefonte; but the difference was that Raider pitcher Tom Burger (6-0) scattered the 11 hits he gave up; and the Tribe's 12 hits off losing pitcher Ken Stewart (2-2) were with men on base, resulting in a 12-4 Bellefonte victory over the Bison.

Clearfield went up 1-0 in the first inning on a Larry Bickle triple and a single by his brother Jerry; but Burger picked a runner off first and struck out a pair.

With two gone in the bottom half of the first, Doug Leathers lined a triple to right center and Doug Hazel followed with a towering home run to left center, giving the Raiders a 2-1 lead.

The Tribe tacked on 3 more runs in the second on a Mike Rhoads single, a walk to Burger, Yogi Leitzell's single, a walk to Doug Sassman, and a Leathers single.

Burger made it 9-1 in the third with a grand-slam home run, driving in Todd Cable, Rhoads, and Terry Cable.

Bellefonte added a run in the fourth on a Hazel single, a wild pitch, and a Mike Watson single; and in the sixth, Larry Saylor walked, Watson singled, and Todd Cable doubled them home.

A 3-run homer by Larry Bickle in the sixth ended the scoring for the Bison.

Robby's Raiders maintained their 2-game lead over Clearfield in the Central Penn League by beating Bald Eagle Area, 7-1, at the Athletic Field in Bellefonte on Tuesday, May 16.

Bellefonte's Tom Burger (7-0) and Bald Eagle's Denny McClure (2-3) both tossed 3-hitters; but the Eagles committed seven errors to the Raiders' one.

The Raiders scored four runs in the second inning on one hit. McClure walked Mike Watson, Todd Cable singled, and two errors allowed two runs to score. Then Yogi Leitzell hit a grounder, forcing one runner; but the return throw was wild, scoring another run and putting men on first and third. Dave Gehret's grounder drove in the fourth run.

In the fifth, a leadoff single by Leitzell, an error, and walks to Watson and Todd Cable accounted for another run.

The Tribe made it 7-0 in the sixth on a leadoff error, another error on Gehret's grounder, and a triple by Larry Saylor.

Bald Eagle, the defending CPL champion, got on the board in the seventh on doubles by Jeff Holter and Dave Kresovich.

Burger, who has won seven of Bellefonte's nine league games, walked one, and struck out seven. Denny McClure walked four and struck out three Raiders.

On Friday, May 19, Bellefonte's Ray McClure (3-0) pitched a 5-hit gem, allowed only one run, walked one, and struck out three in defeating the visiting Mounties of Coach Gerry Davis, 2-1, and clinching a tie for the league title.

Philipsburg got three hits in the first inning, but could only muster one run. After leadoff hitter Dave Lamb bounced out, Rick Osewalt hit a grounder to third; but the throw to first eluded Doug Leathers and Osewalt kept running. In an attempt to nail Osewalt at third, the throw got by Leitzell and Osewalt scored. Consecutive singles by Greg Smeal, Gary Volk, and pitcher Denny Webster (1-1) loaded the bases; but McClure got Barry Covey on a pop fly to third and Barry Miller on a fly ball to center.

Bellefonte threatened in the first and second, but left a pair of runners stranded in both innings. In the sixth, Dave Gehret reached third, but was thrown out at the plate by center fielder Osewalt after tagging up on a Leitzell fly ball.

Todd Cable opened the bottom of the seventh inning with a single inside the bag at third. Larry Saylor hit a swinging bunt in front of the plate which moved Todd to second; and he moved to third on Brother Terry's single. Pitcher Ray McClure grounded to the mound; but Webster's throw to second was on the first base side of the bag, and Terry Cable's slide knocked the ball out of second baseman Barry Covey's glove, filling the bases. Pinch-hitter Gehret drew a walk, forcing in Todd Cable with the tying run. With the outfield pulled in, Yogi Leitzell drilled a single to right center scoring Terry Cable with the winning run.

91

Bellefonte wrapped up its fifth league title in nine years at Lock Haven on Tuesday, May 23, hammering the Bobcats, 15-1.

The Raiders jumped on starter Jim Dugan (1-1) in the first inning, scoring three times. Dave Gehret, filling in for an injured Doug Sassman, led off with a single, stole second, took third on a wild pitch, and came home on a Yogi Leitzell single. Doug Hazel drew a walk, Mike Watson got aboard on an error; and with the bases loaded, Todd Cable hit into a fielder's choice at second, where Watson took out the second baseman and two more runs scored.

Lock Haven scored a run in its half of the first; but the Tribe struck for four more runs in the second. Terry Cable singled, went to second on a passed ball; and after a walk to pitcher Tom Burger, moved to third on a sacrifice by Gehret. Leitzell singled home Cable; and a passed ball, an error on Doug Leathers' grounder, and a two-run single by Watson staked Burger to a 7-1 lead.

Leitzell led the Raider hit parade, going four for four, scoring three times and driving in three runs. Todd Cable had a pair of hits and three RBI's. John Condo was the only 2-hit man for the Bobcats.

Tom Burger (8-0) went five innings, allowed one run on six hits, walked none, and struck out five. Steve Dalena and Frank "Machine Gun" Kelley each pitched an inning and did not allow a hit or a run.

Coach Don Robinson went with his ace, Tom Burger, against Lock Haven in order to clinch the league title on May 23; and Ray McClure pitched well enough to win against Curwensville on Wednesday, May 24; but lacked offensive support in a 5-3 loss in the first round of the District 6 Playoffs.

The Golden Tide of Coach Gary Orwig, a Centre Hall native, got on the board in the first inning. With one out, John Flemming got aboard via an error and Tom Dutry tripled him home. The relay throw skipped past third and out of play, plating Dutry. McClure got a ground-out and a strikeout to end the inning.

The Tribe scored in the bottom of the first when Dave Gehret walked, stole second, and came home on infield outs by Yogi Leitzell and Doug Leathers.

The Tide went up 3-1 in the 2nd on a triple by Ed Passarelli and a Ken Drake hit.

Bellefonte tied it in the third on a walk to McClure, a bunt single by Gehret, a Leitzell sacrifice, an error, and a sac fly by Leathers.

Mike Rhoads led off the fourth with a triple; but died at third after the Tide turned a double play and winning pitcher Todd Wise fanned the next hitter. Curwensville stranded three runners at third and one at second.

The Tide won it in the sixth on a Rick Witherite single, a stolen base, a Dick Howell single, and an error.

Doug Hazel had 2 of the Raider's 6 hits while Passarelli had 2 of the Tide's 7.

Burger pitched one and two-thirds in relief and did not allow a hit or a run.

On Friday, May 26, the Red Raiders bounced back from a disappointing loss to Curwensville at Philipsburg on Wednesday, and finished the season with a 10-0 victory over rival State College at Community Field.

Coach Robinson

It was important to Coach Don Robinson that his team finish on a positive note, and they did just that, pounding out 10 hits off two Little Lion pitchers (Greg Montressor and Tom Fry) and going undefeated in Central Penn League action.

Tom Burger (9-0) pitched a strong game, scattering seven hits while walking only one Lion. He mixed his pitches well and was able to strike out eleven with a curve and slider to go along with his fastball.

The Tribe gave Burger all the support he needed by putting seven runs on the board in the top of the second inning. Three walks, singles by Todd Cable and Mike Watson, a Doug Leathers triple, and a throwing error doomed the Little Lions.

Todd Cable (three for four) and Doug Leathers (two for three) led the Bellefonte offense. Each of them had a triple and produced three RBI's.

Action at third base.

Larry Saylor

93

1972 Bellefonte High School Junior Varsity Team
First Row, L-R: Mike Faulkner, Mark Antolosky, Dave Alterio, Charlie Schrope. **Row 2:** Harry McMurtrie, Jeff Webster, Rick Smalley, Dennis Seaward, Paul Brooks. **Row 3:** Dan Shuey, Dave Hipple, Steve Crowley, Jim Devlin, Jim Musser, Curt Lose, Mike Klinefelter, Don Mulfinger.

The young Red Raiders finished the season with a record of 8-3.
Wins: Penns Valley (4-1 & 15-4); Clearfield (7-6); Bald Eagle (10-5 & 2-0); Philipsburg (4-3 & 6-5); and Lock Haven (14-7).
Losses: Lock Haven (4-2); Clearfield (4-2); and State College (4-0).

In the 1972 season, Coach Robinson came down with a rare affliction by the name of Henoch-Sholein Purpra (HSP), a rash that resembles bruising on the buttocks, feet, and legs; and he ended up in the hospital. One of the doctors finally recognized the ailment, which has no known cause.
Robby was confined to his couch at home for about a week before he could get on his feet and bend his knuckles; and his assistant, Coach Gray took over in his absence. A few ballplayers visited their coach and said things were going fine on the practice field.

1973 Bellefonte High School Varsity Baseball Team

First Row, L-R: Managers Mike Sprankle and Steve Gibboney. **Row 2:** Bill Kovacic, Dave Gehret, Jerry Leitzell, Ray McClure. **Row 3:** Assistant Coach Denny Leathers, Pat Kelly, Al Crafts, Tom Eckley, Dan Shuey, Todd Cable, Coach Don Robinson. **Row 4:** Lenny Young, Gary Drapcho, Larry Saylor, Tom Burger, Steve Crowley, Mike Watson, Charles Riglin, Kenny Grubb.

The Red Raiders won the Central Penn League Championship with an 11-1 record. Wins: State College—9-3 & 7-6; Penns Valley—13-6; Clearfield—1-0 & 19-1; Bald Eagle—4-1 & 13-0; Philipsburg—2-1 & 2-1; Lock Haven—9-0 & 7-0. The only blemish was a 3-2 loss to Penns Valley. The 7-0 win over Lock Haven was a forfeit.

In the 9-3 win over State College on April 10, Tom Burger had 16 strikeouts, scattered 5 hits, and gave up only one free pass. Tom Eckley had a bases-loaded triple, Yogi Leitzell and Todd Cable had 2 hits apiece with 3 RBI's, and Steve Crowley drove in 2 runs with a triple.

On a rainy afternoon in Bellefonte, the Raiders topped Penns Valley 12-6. Ray McClure pitched 4 innings, and gave up 6 hits, 4 runs, and 3 walks. He struck out 5 Rams and got the win. Gary Drapcho pitched the last three innings. Gary Stine took the loss.

On April 17 at Driving Park in Clearfield, rain in the 8th inning stopped a 0-0 battle between the Raiders and the Bison. Tom Burger went the distance giving up 2 hits and striking out 14. Dave Litz went 7 innings for Clearfield and was relieved by Bob Frisco in the eighth.

On April 18, Ray McClure pitched a 1-hitter in a 1-0 victory over Clearfield in the re-match. Bellefonte's lone run came in the 6th inning when Larry Saylor singled, moved to second on McClure's sacrifice bunt, and came home on a clutch double by Dave Gehret. The Raiders loaded the bases, but Danny Heichel relieved Frisco and pitched out of the jam.

In a 9-inning game played at Unionville on April 24, the Tribe stopped the Eagles of Bald Eagle 4-1 as Burger went the distance in recording his second win. Bellefonte scored 3 runs in the 9th aided by a couple of Eagle miscues. One of the errors allowed leadoff hitter Larry Saylor to get aboard; but BEA pitcher Denny McClure retired the next 2 hitters. Mike Rhoads kept the inning going with a single, and Tom Burger's slow roller loaded the bases. A pickoff attempt at third went out of play scoring Saylor and Rhoads. Dave Gehret's single drove in Burger.

Dave Gehret

In a 2-1 win over Philipsburg, Bellefonte Ace Tom Burger got the best of Mountie Ace Chuck Abbott. Both teams were 4-0 going into the game which had been scheduled for April 26; but due to a rainout, the contest was moved to April 30. McClure would have gone against the Mounties; but the postponement gave Tom Burger some needed rest. Philipsburg ace Chuck Abbott had pitched on April 24, so he would not have been ready to face the Raiders on the 26th. However, Coach Gerry Davis elected to go with his second pitcher, Barry Covey, who had a no-hitter to his credit.

In the first inning, Raider Tom Eckley beat out a grounder to third. Yogi Leitzell drilled a single to center and Todd Cable drew a walk to load the bases. Larry Saylor's fly ball to right was lost in the sun by Kip Barnett and dropped in for a single, scoring Eckley. Ken Grubb's grounder to short was bobbled, allowing Leitzell to cross the plate for a second run. Abbott replaced Covey on the mound, and the lefty shut out the Raiders the rest of the way, going six and two-thirds innings, scattering 4 hits and striking out 10.

In the bottom of the first, Jim Wigfield singled, Rick Osewalt walked, and Rich Volk hit a single, scoring Wigfield. With the bases loaded, Bellefonte's defense came up big, as a grounder was hit to Cable, and the shortstop gunned the ball to catcher Saylor for the force out, who in turn fired to first completing a game-saving double play. After that, the game settled down to pitching and defense.

Bellefonte catcher Larry Saylor fires to first, completing a big double play.

In a game at Bellefonte on May 1, the Red Raiders stretched their Central Penn League winning streak to 18 over a 2-year period with a 9-0 victory over Lock Haven. The Bobcats committed 7 errors; but Bellefonte pounded out 10 hits and put crooked numbers on the board in two different innings. Ray McClure tossed a 5-hitter for his third win.

Todd Cable

A second game with Lock Haven resulted in a 7-0 forfeit win for Bellefonte, as the Bobcat seniors were out of school and the underclassmen were taking exams.

On May 3, after State College jumped out to a 5-0 lead over Bellefonte, the Raiders battled back, but trailed 6-4 into the 7th inning. Chuck Riglin, whose previous mound experience was pitching batting practice, took the hill in the 7th and gave up a couple of hits, but did not give up a run. In the bottom of the inning, Cable and Leitzell singled, and Saylor walked to load the bases. Riglin's grounder forced pinch-runner Lenny Young at the plate; and after a strikeout, Mike Watson drew a walk to force in a run. With a full count, Kenny Grubb pounded a walk-off double, driving in Watson and Riglin for a 7-6 victory.

On May 22, Bellefonte crushed Clearfield, 19-1. Don Robinson used the new re-entry rule effectively and correctly in the top of the 6th inning; but Clearfield mentor Sid Lansberry questioned the move and played the game under protest to no avail.

The Tribe jumped on starter Mike Stewart for 3 runs in the 2nd inning; added 5 in the 3rd, 4 more in the 5th, and finished scoring with 7 runs in the 6th inning.

Dave Gehret had two hits, as did Todd Cable, one of which was a double. In the 5th inning, Larry Saylor doubled and scored on a 2-run home run by pinch-hitter Mike Rhoads.

Ray McClure was the winning pitcher, picking up his fourth win against no losses. He went 5 innings, giving up 4 hits, and holding the Bison scoreless. Chuck Riglin pitched the final two innings, allowing two hits and a run.

On May 23, Bellefonte blanked Bald Eagle Area 13-0 and won the Central Penn League Title. The Eagles' Denny McClure, a knuckleball and curve ball pitcher, walked nine and hit a pair of batters. The Raiders scored 2 runs on passed balls.

Ray McClure went 5 innings for Bellefonte and got the win. Harry McMurtrie retired the final 6 Eagles, who had only four base runners all day.

The Bellefonte offense stole the show. Among seven hits were three for extra bases, as the Raiders jumped on a few of Denny McClure's hanging curves.

In the first inning, after Tom Eckley had driven in the first run, Larry Saylor hit a booming home run for a 4-0 Raider lead.

A walk, a passed ball on strike three, and an Eckley single set the stage for a Todd Cable 2-bagger, driving in 3 more runs for a 7-0 advantage.

After two outs in the 5th inning, two Raiders reached base without a hit. Singles by Mike Rhoads and Steve Crowley raised the score to 11-0.

Coach Robinson cleared his bench; but the Raider offense continued to be productive. Lenny Young tripled home Mike Watson, and Young crossed the plate on a passed ball.

Bellefonte beat Philipsburg 2-1 in a home game on May 29. The game was similar to an earlier 2-1 victory over the Mounties. Dave Gehret's first inning fly ball was lost in the sun by right fielder Kip Barnett and Gehret ended up on third. Yogi Leitzell hit a sacrifice fly to left, scoring Gehret. Tom Eckley walked, and Larry Saylor hit a long ball over the shallow Mountie outfield for a triple and a 2-0 Raider lead against lefty ace Chuck Abbott, who pitched hitless ball the rest of the way, allowing only four runners to reach base. Tom Burger, whose arm was hurting, consistently came up with big pitches. He allowed only 5 hits, 1 walk, and struck out ten. In the 6th inning, Barry Miller doubled. Burger struck out the next 3 hitters, but Miller scored when a third-strike pitch got by catcher Larry Saylor.

The Red Raiders of Bellefonte suffered their only defeat of the 1973 season at the hands of Penns Valley by the score of 3-2.

In the Penns Valley game at Millheim, Bellefonte was 11-0; but the Rams, who were 0-11, gave the Raiders their first defeat in the final Central Penn League game of the season. The loss actually helped Bellefonte in the playoffs. On the way back home, Robby told his dejected squad, "We overlooked that Penns Valley team. We were definitely overconfident—just too cocky—and we didn't play to win in that game."

Bellefonte began its quest for a second District VI Title by stopping Curwensville, 6-3, at State College Community Field. Former Centre Hall athlete Gary Orwig's Golden Tide was 11-0 coming into the game.

Curwensville had eliminated Bellefonte from district competition in 1972 with a 5-3 win; and Robby's Raiders got revenge on May 31. The Tide's pitcher, Ken Drake, was as good as anyone the Raiders had faced in the season. However, Bellefonte scored 3 runs in the 3rd inning with 2 outs.

Gary Orwig and Don Robinson

Dave Gehret singled, Yogi Leitzell walked, and a double by Tom Eckley gave Bellefonte pitcher Harry McMurtrie a 2-0 lead. Todd Cable hit a grounder; but Curwensville's first baseman Gearhart failed to touch the bag, and Eckley scored.

The Golden Tide came right back in the top half of the 4th inning with three runs to tie the game. In the bottom of the 4th, Bellefonte had Al Crafts and Steve Crowley on base; but a suicide squeeze attempt failed. Dave Gehret promptly singled home Crowley for a 5-3 lead. In the top of the 5th, Tom Burger took the mound and preserved the Raider lead by pitching three hitless innings as the Tribe added an insurance run.

Claysburg-Kimmel was the next challenge for Bellefonte; and the Raiders met them at Bellwood on June 6. Tom Burger used an off-speed curve to go along with his overpowering fast ball and tamed the Bulldogs, going 7 innings, allowing only a single run on 4 hits, striking out 11 in the 5-1 victory which set up a third meeting with Philipsburg in the district finals. Todd Cable's clutch hit in the first inning put Bellefonte up 1-0. The Raiders scored three times in the 4th off starter Duane Mock. Larry Saylor opened the inning with a double, and consecutive singles by Kenny Grubb, Steve Crowley, and Burger plated a pair. Yogi Leitzell's sacrifice fly accounted for the third tally. In the 5th inning, a Cable walk was followed by singles by Grubb and Al Crafts, scoring Cable. Grubb was the only player to get 2 hits. Claysburg avoided a shutout in the 7th after a one-out free pass and 2 singles.

In a close regular season game at Philipsburg-Osceola, Robby said to a player who was sitting beside him, "I wish I could get more players in the game." The boy's response was that he didn't mind sitting on the bench—he was just happy to be a part of the team.

On June 11, Bellefonte and Philipsburg-Osceola met for the third time in the season—this time in the District VI Championship Game at Penn State's Beaver Field. Mountie Mentor Gerry Davis pointed out the strength of the Central Penn League to have two teams from the league in the finals.

Red Raider ace Tom Burger, the winning pitcher in the both 2-1 victories over Philipsburg in the regular season took the hill.

Burger had a good curve ball to go along with his fast ball, mixed his pitches well, and allowed only two hits in the 3-0 shutout as he out-dueled Mountie ace Chuck Abbott once again. Larry Saylor and Burger each had 2 hits for Bellefonte.

In the first inning, a one-out walk to Yogi Leitzell was followed by a Tom Eckley single; and Todd Cable delivered with a double down the left field line, scoring Eckley and Leitzell. Cable was thrown out at third.

In the bottom half of the inning, Philipsburg had a runner on third with two outs; but Burger got Barry Miller to bounce out to end the threat.

The Raiders added an insurance run in the top of the 5th on a one-out single by Burger, a walk to Dave Gehret, Leitzell's sacrifice, a throwing error on a pickoff attempt by Abbott, and a wild pitch by reliever Barry Covey.

Robby knew what to say to his players at the right time. For example, in the 1973 District VI Championship game against Philipsburg, when pitcher Tom Burger went out for the 7th inning with the Raiders leading 3-0, he told Burger, "You've had a nice two years (16-0), now go out in a blaze of glory. You came into this league as a winner and you should go out as a winner." Burger allowed a leadoff single, but retired the side, giving Robinson his second district title in five years.

At right: Tom Burger

Bellefonte High School 1973 District VI Champions
First Row, L-R: Steve Gibboney, Dave Gehret, Yogi Leitzell, Harry McMurtrie, Bill Kovacic,
Managers Jerry Wert and Mike Sprankle. **Row 2:** District VI Baseball Chairman Jim Sybert,
Coach Don Robinson, Gary Drapcho, Tom Eckley, Ray McClure, Al Crafts, Pat Kelly, Todd
Cable, Assistant Coach Denny Leathers. **Row 3:** Tom Burger, Mike Rhoads, Mike Watson,
Larry Saylor, Steve Crowley, Mike Watson, Kenny Grubb. Absent from photo: Assistant Coach
Ralph Gray, Dan Shuey, Lenny Young, and Charles Riglin.

    The 1973 team was 3-0 in exhibition games with two wins over Tyrone and one
over Altoona.

Honors for the 1973 Red Raiders Baseball Team
James H. Snyder Award: Ray McClure was named the top scholar-athlete at
Bellefonte High School and won the 16th Snyder Award.
Central Penn League All-Stars: Tom Burger, Yogi Leitzell, Todd Cable, and
Tom Eckley.
Altoona Mirror All-Stars: Tom Burger, Tom Eckley, Todd Cable, and Jerry
"Yogi" Leitzell.

OFFICE OF THE

DISTRICT ATTORNEY
CENTRE COUNTY
BELLEFONTE, PA. 16823

June 14, 1973

Mr. Donald Robinson
1131 Centre Street
Bellefonte, Pennsylvania 16823

Dear Robbie:

      Congratulations to you, your staff and your boys for an outstanding baseball season! Winning both the Central Penn championship and the District Six title is a truly fine accomplishment.

      It would be impossible for me to surpass the tributes that have been bestowed upon you in the news media the past several days. Frankly, your 10 year coaching record speaks for itself! Your obvious ability to obtain peak performances from your players game after game attests to your coaching skill and leadership ability.

      It is too bad that baseball does not draw crowds the way football (and even basketball and wrestling) does.

      I am sure that I speak for all fans of baseball -- particularly Bellefonte fans -- when I congratulate you and your team for your skill, competitive spirit and sportsmanship.

Sincerely,

Charles C. Brown, Jr.
District Attorney

Letter of commendation from Chuck Brown, a native of Bellefonte and a Red Raider sports enthusiast. Mr. Brown presently lives in Bellefonte and is a retired Senior Judge of the Centre County Court of Common Pleas in Pennsylvania.

1973 Bellefonte Junior Varsity Baseball Team

First Row, L-R: Manager Dan Rhoads, Britt Smeal, Tom Davidson, Mark Antolosky, Jon Watson, Manager Steve Hartman. **Row 2:** Charlie Schrope, Dave Alterio, Dave Brooks, Harry McMurtrie, Rick Drapcho, Don Mulfinger, Coach Ralph Gray. **Row 3:** Dan Traxler, Rick Smalley, Greg McCartney, Denny Seaward, Jim Musser, Mike Klinefelter, Glenn Fisher, Curt Lose.

Wins: Penns Valley (6-4 & 11-1); Philipsburg (5-3); Clearfield (11-0); Lock Haven (7-0 forfeit); Bald Eagle Area (1-0 & 4-2)
Losses: State College (3-0 & 4-3); Philipsburg (4-3).
Tie: Clearfield (1-1)

Raider pitchers Britt Smeal and Glenn Fisher had a combined 1-hitter in the 11-0 win over Clearfield. Greg McCartney had three hits.

Coach Gray was assisted by volunteer assistant coach John Wetzler.

Jon Watson was at bat, and a pitch came in and hit him. He went to the ground immediately, and when Coach Gray got to him he was still down and moaning in pain. Gray asked him, "Where did it get you?" He replied, "Right in the weenie."

1974 Bellefonte High School Varsity Baseball Team

First Row, L-R: Dan Rhoads, Dan Shuey, Mark Antolosky, Dave Brooks, Charlie Schrope, Barry Williams, Tom Dann, Tom Eckley. **Row 2:** Rick Smalley, Greg McCartney, Dave Houser, Don Mulfinger, Harry McMurtrie, Mike Klinefelter, Rick Drapcho, Coach Don Robinson. **Row 3:** Curt Lose, Gary Drapcho, Steve Crowley, Jim Musser, Larry Saylor, Dan Traxler, Dave Hipple, Denny Seaward.

The Red Raiders compiled an 8-3 record in the Central Penn League with wins over: State College (4-0); Penns Valley (16-3 & 5-1); Clearfield (4-3); Lock Haven (4-3 & 18-7); and Bald Eagle (11-3 & 10-0). Losses were to: State College (5-2); Clearfield (10-1); and Philipsburg (9-1).

The Raiders played seven exhibition games and won four of them. Opponents were Chief Logan, Tyrone, Altoona, and Bald Eagle Nittany. Bald Eagle Nittany, a new addition to the schedule, defeated Bellefonte on a cold April day, knocking the ball all over the place with their aluminum bats. That prompted Coach Robinson to purchase a few of them for his Raiders, adding to their arsenal of wooden bats.

Bellefonte needed a playing field to take on the Chief Logan Mingoes; and the Pleasant Gap field, which paralleled Route 64, was available. Both team busses were parked across the highway from the field, since the playing area extended to the edge of highway. Chief Logan's Coach John Monsell got tossed out of the game; then returned to the team bus where he got atop the vehicle and continued to coach his players from that point.

Monsell was quite a character. When Robby was coaching junior high basketball, Monsell brought his Chief Logan team to the Bellefonte Middle School and the two men conversed prior to the game. Robby asked him what his record was, and Monsell replied, "We're 0-4, including this one."

Monsell coached the last undefeated Chief Logan football team in 1982.

1974 Bellefonte Junior Varsity 11-0 Baseball Team

First row, L-R: Bill Dann, Corky Corrigan, Terry Glunt, Don Holderman. **Row 2:** Jim Shaffer, Tim Glunt, Steve Hoover, Jon Watson, Britt Smeal, Ed Mann. **Row 3:** Coach Ralph Gray, Glenn Fisher, Wes Settle, Tom Hartle, Greg Brown.

Scores:	State College—5-0 & 4-3	Penns Valley—5-3 & 8-1
	Clearfield—5-1 & 9-4	Lock Haven—10-3 & 11-2
	Bald Eagle—7-5 & 5-4	Philipsburg—2-0

As the season's end approached, two of the top junior varsity players, freshmen Dave Houser and Tom Dann, moved up to the varsity. Dann was the winning pitcher against Altoona; and Houser, his battery mate, had a single.

However, the young Raiders picked up the slack and continued to win, finishing the season unbeaten.

1975 Bellefonte High School Varsity Baseball Team

First Row, L-R: Ray Partenheimer, Jon Watson, Greg McCartney, Barry Williams, Harry McMurtrie, Dave Brooks, Mark Antolosky, Dave Alterio, Tom Dann, Dan Rhoads. **Row 2:** Coach Don Robinson, Curt Lose, Denny Seaward, Rick Smalley, Dan Traxler, Jim Musser, Wes Settle, Charlie Schrope, Greg Brown, Dave Houser, Rick Drapcho.

The Raiders ended the season with a 9-6 slate with wins over: Philipsburg (4-3); Bald Eagle Nittany (3-2); Lock Haven (10-3 & 19-0); Clearfield (6-0 & 4-1); Bald Eagle (9-4 & 8-1); and Chief Logan (7-6). Losses came at the hands of: Philipsburg (9-4); State College (14-1 & 2-0); Bald Eagle Nittany (6-5); and Penns Valley (7-2 & 1-0). Bald Eagle Nittany became the eighth member of the Central Penn League in 1975 with former Bellefonte athlete Chuck Casper as head coach.

Harry McMurtrie   **Rick Smalley**   **Dave Alterio**   **Charlie Schrope**

**Left:
Greg
McCartney**

**Center:
Barry
Williams**

**Right:
Curt
Lose**

1975 Bellefonte High School Junior Varsity Team

First Row, L-R: Mark Bush, Don Holderman, Terry Glunt, Steve Adams, Todd McCartney, Ralph Bowersox, Corky Corrigan, Marc Drapcho, Manager Bill Dann. **Row 2:** Coach Ralph Gray, Pat Masullo, Tim Glunt, Jeff Regel, Randy McMullen, Tim Nelson, Neil Teplica, Tom Hartle, Dave Smith, Jim Shaffer, Doug Vonada, Larry Lyons, Volunteer Assistant Coach Bucky Quici.

The Junior Varsity Baseball Team completed its season with 9 wins, 5 losses, and 1 tie. They beat Philipsburg 10-1, Lock Haven 11-3 & 5-3, Penns Valley 9-3, and Clearfield 10-2 & 5-0.

These boys showed a lot of promise for the years to come.

The bus dropped off the Bellefonte boys beyond the outfield of the Bald Eagle Nittany JV Ball Field in Salona when the home team was taking batting practice. As the young Raiders were walking toward their bench along the edge of the playing area, a fly ball came in their direction and hit reserve catcher Ray Bilger on the head. Coach Gray gave the lineup card to his second baseman, Todd McCartney, and told him, "You are now the manager of the team." Gray and Bilger got back on the bus which headed for the Lock Haven Hospital to have the young man checked out. The injury turned out not to be major; but by the time they returned to the ball park, the game was over. When the bus returned to Bellefonte, Coach Gray drove Ray to his home in Pleasant Gap, making sure he got home safely.

World Series: Cincinnati Reds beat the Boston Red Sox 4-3.

College World Series Champion: Texas.

Little League World Champion: Lakewood, New Jersey.

September 16—Rennie Stennett tied Wilbert Robinson's major league record set June 10, 1892, going seven for seven in a 9-inning game.

Jeff Regel

1976

A strong Clearfield team won the Central Penn League Title with two wins over the Raiders (6-5 & 5-3). Penns Valley (10-5), Bald Eagle (7-5) also topped Bellefonte in league play. However, they rang up ten wins, defeating Philipsburg (7-6 & 5-4); Lock Haven (13-2 & 15-8); State College (2-1 & 6-3); Penns Valley (12-1); Bald Eagle (7-5); and Bald Eagle Nittany (8-0 & 4-2).

An excellent Bellefonte team was beaten by Penns Valley at the Athletic Field and the Rams were very excited about beating the Raiders again when they faced them in Millheim in front of 300 fans. Bill Benner was the starting pitcher for the Rams and fanned Bellefonte's first three hitters with a live fastball. In the top of the 2nd, shortstop Greg Brown led off; and Robby told him on his way to the third base coaching box, "You're the guy to get us started." That he did, indeed, as he hit a line drive just past Benner's head which gave the Raiders a big boost of confidence as they won the game with a lot of big hits.

Division I Colleges (including Penn State) and Major League scouts were interested in Tom Dann. "I've been coaching for 14 years and he's the best pitcher I've seen in District 6", according to Coach Don Robinson.

1976 Bellefonte Bench at the Athletic Field

1976 Bellefonte High School Varsity Baseball Team

First Row, L-R: Pat Masullo, John Watson, Ralph Bowersox, Marc Drapcho, Terry Glunt, Jeff Regel, Randy McMullen, Manager Bill Dann, Coach Don Robinson. **Row 2:** Larry Lyons, Don Holderman, Tom Dann, Greg Brown, Wes Settle, Ray Partenheimer, Dave Smith, Dave Houser, Rick Drapcho. Missing from photo: Volunteer Assistant Coach Denny Leathers.

The Raiders finished in a tie with Clearfield for the Central Penn League Title with a 10-4 record, which necessitated a league playoff game won by Clearfield, 8-1. However, the Tribe proceeded to win the District 6 AAA Title with wins over Altoona (8-4) and Hollidaysburg (5-0). Bellefonte pitcher Tom Dann was masterful in the final game with Hollidaysburg, as the Tiger batters took strike after strike against the Raider ace. After the game, Tiger Assistant Coach Jim Hancuff said their players were caught looking so often due to the fact that they had not seen a pitcher as good as Dann.

A 2-1 record in exhibition play gave Bellefonte a slate of 14-6 for the season.

In 1976, the Junior Varsity season had come to an end, and Coach Gray joined Robby with the varsity team, bringing along a couple of JV players for a crucial game at Bald Eagle Nittany. One of the young ballplayers was Tim Nelson, who was blessed with great speed. In the late innings in a close contest, at the suggestion of Coach Gray, Robby inserted Nelson to pinch-run at first base; and he got picked off rather quickly. Robby's reaction was, "There is no question about his speed—it only took him 15 seconds to get picked off."

Fortunately, the Raiders pulled out a 4-2 win over Bald Eagle Nittany with a 3-run rally with two out in the last inning. A triple by Tom Dann was the big blow that enabled Bellefonte to keep pace with Clearfield.

The playoff game with Clearfield for all the marbles in the Central Penn League was scheduled for Friday, May 28, at Philipsburg. Meanwhile, on Thursday, May 27, Bellefonte took on Altoona in a semi-final game for the District 6 AAA Championship at the Athletic Field.

Coach Don Robinson decided to go with left-handed pitcher Tom Dann against Jay Perry's Mountain Lions, a big, strong team that might hit Don Holderman pretty hard. He felt Holderman, a righty, would be more effective against Clearfield, which was heavily stocked with right-handed hitters.

Dann was able to overpower Altoona, striking out 12, including six after two innings. He surrendered eight hits, four runs, and walked four in seven innings for an 8-4 Bellefonte victory.

The Raiders jumped on Altoona starter Chris Cobo for six runs in the second inning. Pat Masullo led off with a single; and after Wes Settle popped out, Dann drew a walk and Randy McMullen singled to load the bases. Rick Drapcho, hitting ninth in the lineup, blooped a single to right scoring Masullo. Terry Glunt lined a single to center to drive in Dann and a wild pitch brought in McMullen with the third run, putting runners on second and third. Jeff Regel hit a bouncer to third and third baseman Brian Franco made a throw to home. However, Drapcho was not running on the play, and all the Altoona catcher could do was watch Regel cross the first base bag, loading the bases.

Dave Houser promptly lined a single to left that got by outfielder Bob Stout, and two more runners crossed the plate. Regel was thrown out at home, but Houser moved to third on the play and scored on a Cobo wild pitch. Cobo was injured in a collision with Houser at the plate and was replaced with Mike Nagle.

The Mountain Lions scored two runs in the top of the third on a homer by Joe Holsinger and added isolated runs in the fifth and seventh.

Dann led off the third with a single and McMullen moved him to third with a double that bounced over the fence in left-center. With one out and Glunt at the plate, Coach Robinson called for a suicide squeeze. Dann was halfway home when Nagle released the ball, and Glunt never had a chance to get the bat on the ball because catcher Jeff Franco reached in front of the plate, whereupon umpire Jake Salsgiver ruled catcher's interference, sending Glunt to first and awarding bases to both Dann and McMullen.

Coach Perry argued to no avail, and Houser promptly singled home McMullen for the eighth Raider run.

Houser went two for four on the day with three RBI's. McMullen, hitting in the eighth spot, had three hits in four at-bats and scored two runs. Dann was two for three with two runs scored.

On Friday, May 28, Clearfield beat Bellefonte, 8-1 in a playoff game for the CPL title at Philipsburg. In the two regular season's meetings, Clearfield prevailed in close games that took 21 innings to decide the winner.

All season long, the Tribe relied on pitching, tight defense, and clutch hitting; but on this day, all three qualities were non-existent. The Bison pounded Raider starter Don Holderman for 11 hits and 8 runs; and the Raider defense committed 5 errors. A well-rested Mike McNamee went the distance for Clearfield, scattering six hits and walking none while striking out three.

The Bison got on the board in the first inning when Jeff Norris reached first on an error, took second on a sacrifice, moved to third on another error, and scored on a passed ball.

After one out in the second, Sid Lansberry's lads plated three more runs. Doug Trude got aboard on an error, Garry Shirey's fielder's choice erased Trude; but McNamee stroked a single, Jeff Norris doubled to the fence for two runs, and Rick Schickling singled home Norris.

In the fourth, the Bison added two runs on singles by Norris, Randy Zortman, Bob Fargo, Dave Pry, and Tom Flanagan.

Bellefonte avoided a shutout in the fourth. Greg Brown reached first on a fielder's choice and scored on a triple by Tom Dann.

Clearfield finished its scoring with two in the fifth. Shirey doubled, Norris singled following McNamee's sacrifice, and Schickling doubled in Norris. An error put Zortman on first, and Fargo flied to Dann in right, who nailed Schickling at the plate for the inning-ending out.

Norris and Schickling had three hits apiece for Clearfield and Fargo added two more. Dave Houser and Terry Glunt each had two hits for the Tribe.

Marc Drapcho took the hill for the final two and two-thirds innings and allowed two hits, no runs, walked one, and struck out two Bison batters.

November 5—New American League franchises in Seattle and Toronto.

On Wednesday, June 2, the Raiders of Coach Don Robinson ended their season with a District 6 AAA Championship by defeating Hollidaysburg, 5-0 at Bellefonte's Athletic Field.

Raider pitcher Tom Dann was dominant in a game that took only one hour and 10 minutes to complete. He mixed his curve and fast ball well and got ahead of the hitters. Most of his 14 strikeouts were on a 1-2 count.

Dann drew praise from Hollidaysburg Coach Pat Cummings, as the junior lefty had a perfect game going into the fifth inning. A bloop single to the opposite field by Marty Culp ruined the no-hitter; but Dann did not ease up or lose his concentration over the final pair of innings and did not walk a batter.

Dann struck out the side in the first, third, and seventh innings and got seven of the first nine batters he faced on strikes.

Bellefonte went on top, 1-0, in the first inning when Wes Settle reached on a fielder's choice that forced Greg Brown at second. One out later, Pat Masullo and Randy McMullen singled back to back, scoring Settle.

The Tribe added on in the third when Terry Glunt led off with a walk and scored one out later on Dave Houser's triple. After Brown popped up, Settle drew a walk and Tiger pitcher Scott Love balked when Settle left early on a delayed steal, and Houser was awarded home, making the score 3-0.

The other Raider runs were tacked on in the sixth on a Settle single, an error on Dann's sacrifice bunt, two more Hollidaysburg errors, and a Masullo single. Masullo had two hits and three RBI's on the day.

Houser also had two hits, giving him 35 for the season in 79 at-bats for a .443 average. Twenty-nine of his hits were singles; and the switch-hitter scored 20 runs, had 23 RBI's, and had a perfect fielding average for the season.

All the starters will be back for the 1977 season, except center fielder Rick Drapcho, who will graduate. **Below: 1976 Bellefonte Bench, L-R:**

Coach Gray, Ken Grubb, Coach Robinson, Steve Adams, Mark Bush, Ralph Bowersox.

1976 Bellefonte High School Junior Varsity Team
First Row, L-R: Steve Adams, Mike Sheckler, Todd McCartney, Scott Smith, Bryan Rhoads, Rob Bonneau, Fred Wilson. **Row 2:** Coach Ralph Gray, Jeff Stover, Ray Bilger, Mark Robbins, Darren Lutz, Don Drapcho, Doug Vonada. Absent from picture: Mark Bush, Tim Nelson, and Volunteer Assistant Coach Jack Stover.

The pitching of Doug Vonada and Nick Hrabowenski contributed to a successful season for the JV team. The Raiders finished in a first-place tie with Clearfield with an 11-3 record.

World Series: Cincinnati Reds beat the New York Yankees, 4-0.

College World Series Champion: Arizona.

Little League World Series Champion: Chofu, Tokyo, Japan.

Philadelphia Phillies won the Eastern Division with a record of 101-61
.

August 9—John Candelaria became the first Pirate pitcher in 69 years to throw a no-hitter in Pittsburgh in beating the Los Angeles Dodgers, 2-0. The game was played in Three Rivers Stadium. No Pirate ever threw a no-hitter at Forbes Field.

November 29—Reggie Jackson signs with the New York Yankees for $3.5 million.

1977 Bellefonte High School Varsity Baseball Team
Central Penn League Champions
District VI Champions

First Row, L-R: Jeff Regel, Marc Drapcho, Todd McCartney, Ralph Bowersox, Terry Glunt, Steve Adams, Jim Shaffer. **Row 2:** Ray Bilger, Pat Masullo, Doug Vonada, Tom Dann, Larry Lyons, Darren Lutz, Mark Bush. **Row 3:** Coach Don Robinson, Dave Smith, Greg Brown, Wes Settle, Dave Houser, Randy McMullen, Assistant Coach Ralph Gray. Absent from photo: Don Holderman, Bryan Rhoads.

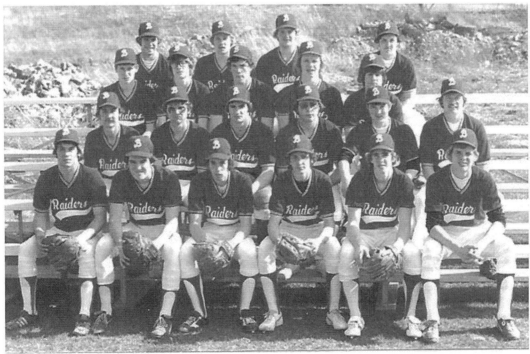

1977 Bellefonte High School Varsity Baseball Team
Row 1, L-R: Mark Bush, Doug Vonada, Ralph Bowersox, Todd McCartney, Terry Glunt, Don Holderman. **Row 2:** Marc Drapcho, Jim Shaffer, Jeff Regel, Darren Lutz, Steve Adams, Coach Don Robinson. **Row 3:** Ken Grubb, Dave Smith, Greg Brown, Randy McMullen, Pat Masullo. **Row 4:** Tom Dann, Dave Houser, Wes Settle, Doug Vonada.

The 1977 Red Raiders compiled an excellent record of 20-3. The only Central Penn League loss was to Philipsburg-Osceola, and they lost in an exhibition game to Chief Logan. Hatboro-Horsham, the eventual state champion, pinned the final loss on the Raiders, 3-1, in the PIAA Tournament in Shippensburg.

Regular season wins: Altoona (8-2); Lewistown (6-5); Tyrone (14-4); Bald Eagle Area (14-3 & 9-7); Bald Eagle Nittany (14-3 & 9-7); Philipsburg (7-1); Lock Haven (13-0 & 12-3); State College (4-1 & 9-0); Penns Valley (11-2 & 2-0); and Clearfield (5-2 & 6-3).

District VI Playoff wins: Indiana (3-2); State College (3-0); and West Branch (11-0).

P.I.A.A. State Tournament win: Valley View (10-5).

The first three home games (Lewistown, Tyrone, and Bald Eagle Area) were played at the Bellefonte Teener Field since the Athletic Field was not playable.

The Raider pitching staff in 1977 was led by Tommy Dann with a 14-1 record. Darren Lutz was 5-0, followed by Donny Holderman 1-1 and Marc Drapcho 0-1. Their ERA was 1.61 and the strike-out-walk ratio was 4.76.

The team hit .327; had an on-base percentage of .595; averaged 9.0 hits/game; 7.4 runs /game; hit 27 home runs; and had a fielding average of .927.

The 1977 Season in Brief

Wednesday, March 30—Bellefonte 8, Altoona 2 @ Mansion Park in Altoona. Wes Settle had a triple. Greg Brown and Tom Dann had 2 hits apiece. Tom Dann pitched 7 innings, gave up 3 hits, no earned runs, and struck out 15 for his first win. The Tribe knocked out the Mountain Lion starter in the first, scoring 5 runs on singles by Dann and Dave Smith and a bases-loaded walk to Randy McMullen. **At right: Tom Dann and Jeff Regel.**

Thursday, March 31—Bellefonte 6, Lewistown 5 @ Bellefonte Teener Field. Jim Shaffer had a home run and Jeff Regel had 2 hits. Pitcher Don Holderman went 7 innings, allowed 5 hits, 1 earned run, and struck out 10 for his first win. The Raiders had six miscues.

Friday, April 1—Bellefonte 14, Tyrone 4 @ Bellefonte Teener Field. Steve Adams, Jeff Regel, and Pat Masullo homered. Greg Brown had 2 hits. Doug Vonada went 3 innings, gave up 5 hits, 4 earned runs, and struck out 1. Darren Lutz picked up his first win in relief, allowing 2 hits, no runs, and striking out 3 in his 4 innings pitched.

Thursday, April 7—Bellefonte 14, Bald Eagle 3 @ Bellefonte Teener Field. Jeff Regel had 2 home runs; and Tom Dann, Pat Masullo, and Jim Shaffer homered. Dave Smith had 3 hits. Winning pitcher was Tom Dann (2-0); he went 6 innings, gave up 4 hits, 3 earned runs, and struck out 11. Darren Lutz pitched one inning, allowed 3 hits, no runs, and struck out one hitter. Eagle Coach Alex Murnyack complained about the short outfield fence; but Robby pointed out it was the same distance for both teams.

Monday, April 11—Bellefonte 5, Bald Eagle Nittany 0 @ Mill Hall. Jim Shaffer had a home run, Wes Settle had 3 hits; and Jeff Regel and Shaffer each had 2. Tom Dann (3-0) pitched a no-hitter in his seven innings of shutout baseball and struck out 15.

Tuesday, April 12—Philipsburg-Osceola 8, Bellefonte 4 @ Bellefonte. The Raiders had 6 hits which included doubles by Wes Settle and Jeff Regel. Pitcher Don Holderman (1-1) went 5 innings and took the loss. He gave up 7 hits, 3 earned runs, and struck out 2. Darren Lutz in relief allowed 3 hits, one earned run and struck out 2. The Raiders had six errors.

Thursday, April 14—Bellefonte 13, Lock Haven 0 @ Lock Haven. Jeff Regel, Pat Masullo, and Wes Settle hit home runs. Right fielder Marc Drapcho had 3 hits, while Settle, Regel, and Randy McMullen had two. Tom Dann (4-0) was the winning pitcher. He went 5 innings, allowed 2 hits, no runs, and struck out 11. Darren Lutz pitched 2 hitless innings and struck out 4 Bobcats.

Tom Dann

Tuesday, April 19—Bellefonte 4, State College 1 @ Community Field in State College. The Raiders banged out 7 hits. Tom Dann (5-0) was masterful, allowing only 2 hits, no earned runs, and struck out 12 in his 7 innings.

Thursday, April 21—Bellefonte 11, Penns Valley 2 @ Bellefonte. Jeff Regel and Dave Houser each had a double and two singles, and Greg Brown added a 2-bagger. Starting pitcher Marc Drapcho put zeros on the board in his one inning and struck out 2. Darren Lutz (2-0) went the remaining six frames, allowing 2 runs on 5 hits, and striking out 7. The Raiders improved their league record to 5-1.

Friday, April 22—Chief Logan 9, Bellefonte 6 @ the Athletic Field in Bellefonte. Pat Masullo and Randy McMullen had 2 hits apiece, while Jim Shaffer had the only other safety. The Mingoes jumped on starter Marc Drapcho (0-1) in the first inning, and scored seven times on 3 hits and 3 free passes without recording an out. Tom Dann relieved Drapcho, and allowed 2 runs (one earned), 4 hits, and struck out 12 in his seven innings. Bellefonte's overall record became 8-2 with the loss.

Tuesday, April 26—Bellefonte 5, Clearfield 2 @ Clearfield. Jeff Regel and Tom Dann each had 2 hits in defeating the Bison. Tom Dann gave up 5 hits, one earned run, and struck out 15 en route to his sixth consecutive win. The Raiders had 9 hits and improved their league record to 6-1.

Thursday, April 28—Bellefonte 10, Bald Eagle Nittany 0 @ Bellefonte. The game ended with two outs in the 5th inning, as the 10-run rule was invoked. Greg Brown, Dave Houser, Wes Settle, and Randy McMullen had eight of the Raider's ten hits. Brown, Houser, and Steve Adams had doubles, and Settle hit a home run. Pitcher Darren Lutz (3-0) scattered 4 hits and struck out 4.

1977 Bellefonte Bench

Tuesday, May 3—Bellefonte 9, Bald Eagle Area 7 @ Wingate. The Raiders pounded out 12 hits as Greg Brown and Dave Houser led the way with 3 hits each. Pat Masullo had 2 singles as the Tribe went into a first-place tie with Philipsburg. Starter Don Holderman pitched 5 innings, allowing 7 runs (3 earned) and struck out 4. Tom Dann (7-0) gave up only 2 hits in 3 innings of relief and got the win.

Friday, May 6—Bellefonte 7, Philipsburg 1 @ Philipsburg. The Raiders took sole possession of first place in the league as Tom Dann (8-0) pitched a 2-hitter and struck out 16 Mounties. The Tribe had 10 hits as Dave Houser, Wes Settle, and Pat Masullo each had a pair. Settle had a 2-bagger and Bellefonte was perfect in the field.

Tuesday, May 10—Bellefonte 12, Lock Haven 3 @ Bellefonte. Dave Houser had 3 hits, Jeff Regel and Greg Brown had 2 apiece. Brown's homer was the only extra base hit in the Raiders' 10 safeties. Darren Lutz (4-0) went the distance, allowing 5 hits, 2 earned runs, and striking out 7 Bobcats.

Thursday, May 12—Bellefonte 9, State College 0 @ Bellefonte. The leading hitter for the Raiders was Greg Brown with 3, two of which were home runs. Dave Houser had 2 of the Tribe's 5 singles and Jeff Regel had a double. Tom Dann (9-0) scattered four Little Lion hits and struck out 17.

Tuesday, May 17—Bellefonte 2, Penns Valley 0 @ Penns Valley. The Tribe had 8 hits including Greg Brown's 2, one of which was a homer. Darren Lutz (5-0) only allowed 2 hits in his four and a third innings and struck out 4. In relief, Tom Dann did not allow a hit and struck out 6 Rams in his two and two-thirds innings.

Thursday, May 19—Bellefonte 6, Clearfield 4 @ Bellefonte. The Raiders captured the Central Penn League Championship with the win and a 13-1 CPL record.   Pat Masullo had 2 singles, while Wes Settle had a double and a home run. The Tribe banged out 8 hits and had only one error in the field. Tom Dann (10-0) allowed only 4 Bison bingles, 3 earned runs, and struck out 10. The Raiders ran their overall record to 16-2.

At right: Dave Houser on base in the State College game.

Coach Robinson   Coach Gray   **On Deck Hitters—Left to Right: Terry Glunt, Pat Masullo, Ralph Bowersox**

Leadoff hitter Terry Glunt had an on-base average of .604.

Shortstop Ralph Bowersox had a fielding average of .860.

Junior Pat Masullo had a batting average of .377 and fielding average of .925.

Robby's Raiders had a team fielding average of .927.

Wes Settle led the team in runs-batted-in with 25.

Greg Brown led the team in hits (28) and singles (20).

Dave Houser led the team in hitting with an average of .442.

1977 Seniors
(Batting Average)
First Row, L-R:
Terry Glunt (.250)
Tom Dann (.347)
Marc Drapcho (.185)
Jim Shaffer (.307)

Row 2:
Dave Smith (.280)
Greg Brown (.383)
Wes Settle (.372)
Dave Houser (.442)
Larry Lyons (.250)

Wes Settle led the team in RBI's with 25. Greg Brown, who was the first pro player in Don Robinson's 15 years of coaching, was second in home runs with 5. Junior Jeff Regel had 6.

"Greg Brown is the best hitting prospect I've ever seen in high school", stated Raider Coach Don Robinson.

New York Mets scout Jocko Collins, who signed Brown to a pro contract, had a similar opinion, "What stood out was that he's a pretty darn good hitter and I think he's going to be a heck of a hitter."

Local players Ray Cingle, Bo Sankey, Cal Emery, Ed Drapcho, Bob Luse, and Denny Leathers signed professional baseball contracts. Drapcho pitched for Benny Benford and the Bellefonte Red Raiders.

At age 18, Denny Leathers signed with the Philadelphia Phillies, and pitched four seasons of professional baseball, ending up in the San Francisco Giant organization in 1968. A knee injury ended his professional career; but he became a star in the Centre County League and was elected to the first Centre County Sports Hall of Fame in 2017.

He got his college degree and began teaching social studies at the Bellefonte Middle School in 1970.

Leathers was hired as an assistant baseball coach and worked with Coach Don Robinson in 1971-73, and 1979-81. He became the head coach in 1982 and won nine Central Penn League Titles and five District VI Championships in his 30 years at the helm. He coached Eric Milton, a Bellefonte boy who became a major league pitcher. **At right: Denny Leathers.**

Robby and Indiana Coach Bob Baden

District VI Playoffs

In the 3-2 playoff victory over Indiana High School at Bellefonte, Darren Lutz, who was 5-0 on the season, went four and a third innings giving up only one earned run against the 14-3 Little Indians. However, the Raiders were trailing, 2-1 when Tom Dann relieved Lutz in the 5th; but he got a strikeout and ground out to end the inning.

Dann struck out the side in the 6th inning; and the Raiders tied the game in the bottom of the frame when Steve Adams doubled home Mark Bush, a pinch-runner for Pat Masullo, who led off the 6th with a double. In the 7th, Dann picked off the leadoff batter who had walked, and struck out the last 2 hitters. In the bottom of the inning, Wes Settle singled home Greg Brown for the win.

The night before the game, Robby went over to Assistant Coach Ralph Gray's home and they discussed the possibility of starting Lutz instead of

Dann. If Dann had pitched against Indiana he wouldn't have been available to go against State College the next day in the District VI AAA final at Beaver Field. On game day, Indiana did not look like the same team that warmed up prior to Tuesday's game that was rained out[6]. So Robby went with Darren Lutz.

At left: Raider second baseman Terry Glunt goes high in the air to stop a throw from catcher Jeff Regel, as Indiana's Al McCormick slides safely into second.

---

[6] The postponed game could not be played on Wednesday due to an awards banquet that was scheduled in Indiana.

Friday, May 27—Bellefonte 3, State College 0 @ Penn State's Beaver Field. The Raiders copped the District 6 AAA Title by defeating State College for the third time in the season. The Tribe had only 3 hits off loser Terry Curley—Jeff Regel (double), Wes Settle (single), and Jim Shaffer (double). Settle drove in 2 runs. Tom Dann (12-0) pleased the large Bellefonte delegation by pitching a 2-hitter and striking out 10 Little Lions.

Jeff Regel

Thursday, June 2—Bellefonte 11, West Branch 0 @ Penn State's Beaver Field in State College. In a battle of Indians, the Bellefonte Tribe was superior, collecting 11 hits and winning the 5-inning game via the 10-run rule. Terry Glunt had 2 singles and Tom Dann added a single and a double. Jeff Regel and Pat Masullo hit round trippers. Dann (13-0) pitched his second no-hitter of the season and struck out 10. The Raiders were perfect in the field.

A large crowd gathered at Penn State's Beaver Field for the game with West Branch, which would determine the team to represent District 6 in the first state tournament at Shippensburg. Larry Dobo, an outstanding pitcher, was on the hill; and he was opposed by Bellefonte ace, Tommy Dann. Raiders Pat Masullo and Jeff Regel hit back-to-back homeruns and Regel's was a grand slam. Bellefonte athletic director Bill Luther grabbed a batting helmet; and with the crowd still on its feet, passed the "hat" and collected donations for the team's trip to Shippensburg.

Photo at left:

Red Raider Coach Don Robinson (center) discusses the re-scheduling of the 1977 P.I.A.A. Playoff game between Bellefonte and Valley View with a tournament official (right) in Shippensburg while Centre Daily Times sports writer Ron Bracken (left) listens in on the proceedings.

Raider Coach Don Robinson accepts a check from Wayne Koch, President of the Bellefonte Teachers Association, for the baseball team to make the trip to Shippensburg for the P.I.A.A. State Tournament. Next to Robinson is Assistant Coach Ralph Gray and Matt Chadwick, association vice-president.

Word got around the Bellefonte Community that the baseball team needed funds to make the trip to Shippensburg to represent District 6 in the very first P.I.A.A. State Baseball Tournament.

Baseball fans began coming up to the high school office to donate money so the team could make the well-earned trip.

Bellefonte High School's Athletic Director, Bill Luther, had a morning sports show on station WBLF in Bellefonte, and he made an appeal to the community to support the baseball team in its quest for a state title.

The money poured in for a couple of weeks; and due to the strong support of the town's baseball fans, the 1977 Red Raiders were able to go to Shippensburg in style.

Bill Luther

Tom Dann

In the first round of the P.I.A.A. Baseball Tournament, Bellefonte defeated the Valley View Cougars 10-5, as Tom Dann, despite 7 walks, gave up only 4 hits and struck out 12.

The game was originally scheduled for Thursday, June 9; but a rainout forced it to be rescheduled for Friday at 9 a.m.

Valley View's ace Gary Cocetti, who like Dann, was 13-0 coming into the contest, wasn't sharp as the Raiders pounded him for 5 hits and 4 runs. He was relieved by John Jones, who gave up 9 hits and 6 runs. Dann, Terry Glunt, Greg Brown, Dave Houser, Pat Masullo each had 2 hits; and Jeff Regel led the Tribe with 3 safeties. Wes Settle had a homer and 3 RBI's.

In a bizarre bottom of the first, Glunt led off with a walk, and moved to second on Brown's one-out single. An error on Houser's grounder loaded the bases. Settle hit a grounder to third and Glunt was forced at home. Masullo took a third call strike on a 3-2 count, and the ball popped out of catcher Jerry Papabelli's glove. Instead of firing to first for an easy out, he rolled the ball back to the mound as the Valley View fielders walked off the field; and Bellefonte runners Brown and Houser scored on the play. Cougar Coach Gary Ceccarelli argued to no avail that the ball had not been dropped.

World Series: New York Yankees over the Los Angeles Dodgers, 4-2.

College World Series Champion: Arizona State.

Little League World Champions: Li-Teh, Kaohsiuna, Taiwan.

Dave Parker of the Pittsburgh Pirates won the National League batting title with a .338 average.

After eliminating Valley View in the morning of June 10, Bellefonte met one of the top tournament seeds in the afternoon in Hatboro-Horsham, a Quad-A school that received a first round bye.

At a meeting of the coaches and director of the tournament, someone asked why the AAAA schools got byes. He replied, "Because they were the biggest schools."

At left: Raider second baseman Todd McCartney forces a Hatboro-Horsham runner.

Hatboro ended Bellefonte's season with a 3-1 decision and went on to become the State Baseball Champion. Two of their runs scored on similar plays:
In the bottom of the first inning, Dave Simononis (who went on to Penn State) and Kevin Quirk both singled off Tom Dann, who was pitching his second game of the day. Merle Palmer hit a grounder between first and second that was fielded by first baseman Pat Masullo, who tossed the ball to Dann, who was covering first. While Dann was disputing the safe call, Simononis kept running and scored from second base. In the 3rd inning, Simononis was on second base with two outs. Palmer again hit a grounder in the hole at second, which was fielded by Masullo, and he tossed the ball to Dann who was covering first. Palmer was ruled safe again; and again while Dann was arguing the call, Simononis kept running and Hatboro went up, 2-1. The next batter, Bob Bolger, hit a grounder to third, but the errant throw eluded Masullo at first; and Palmer, who was off with the crack of the bat, scored to make it 3-1.

The Raiders had a great opportunity in the 2nd inning. Hatboro hurler Wayne Sands got wild and walked Dave Houser, Ralph Bowersox, and Wes Settle to load the bases with nobody out. Sands got Masullo on a short fly to left. Dann hit a fly ball to center and Houser was able to tag up and score. The right-hander then struck out Todd McCartney to end the inning.

Sands was masterful with a great drop to go along with his fastball. He went the distance, allowing only 3 hits, and striking out 11.

Tom Dann held the 20-2 District 1 Champions from the Philadelphia area to 5 hits and 3 runs; and struck out 6 in his 5 innings. Darren Lutz pitched the 6th and did not allow a hit.

125

Coach Don Robinson had no choice as to who was going to pitch against Hatboro-Horsham. Dann would not have been able to go the next day and Robinson had to save Lutz for that game.

Dann said he could pitch again on the same day because he once went 17 innings in an American Legion game. He iced his arm in a whirlpool tub between games and actually felt stronger at the beginning of the second game.

Strategy meeting in the sixth inning of the Hatboro-Horsham game

Left to right: Catcher Jeff Regel, Third Baseman Randy McMullen, Coach Don Robinson, Shortstop Ralph Bowersox, Pitcher Darren Lutz, Second Baseman Todd McCartney, and First Baseman Pat Masullo.

Randy McMullen, Todd McCartney, and Darren Lutz each singled for the only Raider hits off Wayne Sands.

Going into the game, Tom Dann was 14-0 and Wayne Sands was 8-0.

126

1977 Bellefonte High School Junior Varsity Team
First Row, L-R: Scott Smith, Bill O'Neill, Tim Wilson, Randy Martz, Alan Luther, Ron Lidgett. **Row 2:** Bryan Rhoads, Don Drapcho, Chris Burger, Dave Witmer, Armond Aquilino, Jeff Stover, Coach Ralph Gray.

The Philadelphia Phillies won the Eastern Division title with a record of 101-61.

April 15—The Montreal Expos played their first game at Montreal's Olympic Stadium. The Phillies won the game, 7-2.

May 30—Dennis Eckersley threw a no-hitter as Cleveland beat the California Angels, 1-0.

June 29—Willie Stargell of the Pirates hit his 400th home run as Pittsburgh beat the St. Louis Cardinals, 9-1.

October 18—In game six of the World Series, Reggie Jackson went 3 for 3 with three home runs in an 8-4 New York Yankee victory.

November 2—Steve Carlton of the Phillies won his second Cy Young Award. He won 23 games.

1978 Bellefonte High School Varsity Baseball Team

First Row, L-R: Managers Chris Lehman, David Ivicic, Barry Reese. **Row 2:** Steve Adams, Chris Burger, Cameron White, Doug Smith, Don Drapcho, Randy Martz, Scott Smith, Armond Aquilino. **Row 3:** Mark Bush, Brian Tressler, Ray Bilger, Ralph Bowersox, Randy McMullen, Pat Masullo, Todd McCartney, Jeff Regel, Nick Hrabowenski, Doug Vonada, Coach Don Robinson.

The Red Raiders finished the regular season with a 14-5 record. Wins were over Altoona (7-4); Tyrone (4-3); Chief Logan (7-2), Lewistown (13-3); Bald Eagle Nittany (16-6 & 11-1); Philipsburg (12-11 &5-1); Bald Eagle (2-1 & 10-0); State College (5-3 & 7-2); and Penns Valley (7-1 & 4-1). Losses: Clearfield (7-3 & 11-3); Lock Haven (3-2 & 7-4); and Chief Logan (8-4).

In District VI action, Bellefonte defeated State College for the third time, 7-2; and its season ended with an 8-3 loss to Philipsburg.

There was only one television set in the Gray home in Bellefonte; and Ralph liked to watch major league baseball in the evening. If his children, Natalie and Bill wanted to watch TV, they had to watch baseball. To keep them interested, he gave each of them a scorebook and taught them to keep score of the game. Natalie's ability to keep a scorebook paid off in the 1978 season, as she became the scorekeeper for the Bellefonte Varsity Baseball Team.

1978 Bellefonte High School Junior Varsity Baseball Team
First row, L-R: Ron Lidgett, Greg McMullen, Bill Masullo, Alan Luther. **Row 2:** John Zelenky, Charlie Baney. **Row 3:** Mike Surovec, Tim Wion, Scott Witmer, Ron Tressler, Carl Deitrich. **Row 4:** Coach Ralph Gray, Shane Settle, Dick Tressler, Tim Wilson, Wes Gates, Denny Sweeny, Greg Murray.

The JV's had a record of 11-4; and that marked the fifth consecutive season the team won ten or more games.

Victories: Chief Logan (9-8 & 3-1); Bald Eagle Nittany (10-0 & 6-5); Philipsburg-Osceola (14-1 & 13-2); State College (4-1); Lock Haven (8-1 & 6-1); and Penns Valley (11-3 & 12-3).

Losses: Bald Eagle Area (7-6 & 8-6); Clearfield (7-5); and State College (9-5).

1979 Bellefonte High School Varsity Baseball Team
First Row, L-R: Bill Masullo, Doug Smith, Bryan Rhoads, Bill O'Neill, Randy Martz, Tim Wilson, Scott Smith, Wes Gates, Manager Dave Ivicic. **Row 2:** Assistant Coach Ralph Gray, Don Drapcho, Armond Aquilino, Chris Burger, Jim Scheaffer, Scott Witmer, Cameron White, Dick Tressler, Alan Luther, Greg McMullen, Coach Don Robinson.

For the 1979 season, Assistant Coach Ralph Gray moved up to the varsity; and Assistant Coach Denny Leathers took over the JV program.

The Red Raiders continued their winning tradition, finishing the season with a record of 10 and 7. Senior Doug Smith led the team in hitting with an average of .315; and Bryan Rhoads had a 4-0 record on the mound.

Victories: Philipsburg (6-4 & 10-0); Bald Eagle Nittany (8-6 & 6-5); Lock Haven (6-3 & 6-1); Clearfield (4-3); Bald Eagle Area (4-1 & 3-1); and Penns Valley (13-5). Defeats: Lewistown (6-4); Altoona (6-2); Penns Valley (2-1); State College (3-1 & 10-5); Clearfield (18-6); and Chief Logan (8-7).

At Left: Coach Don Robinson takes pre-game infield practice.

On one occasion Robby was taking pre-game infield, and the guys didn't look sharp. Their throws were off the mark and they were mishandling ground balls. He suddenly said, "That's enough", and abruptly ended the practice and sent the players to the bench. He then told them, "Pre-game infield is for show. If we can't look good, we're not going to do it."

130

Seniors

D. Drapcho

R. Martz

D. Smith

S. Smith

C. White

1979 Bellefonte High School Varsity Baseball Seniors
Don Drapcho, Randy Martz, Doug Smith, Scott Smith, Cameron White.

1979 Bellefonte High School Junior Varsity Baseball Team

First Row, L-R: Doug Ishler, Mike Mann, Charlie Baney, Dean Gentzel. **Row 2:** Jake Corman, Geoff Kline, Ron Surovec, Dave Bernhard, Randy Wright, Carl "Chip" Deitrich, Mike Surovec. **Row 3:** Coach Denny Leathers, Denny Sweeny, Greg Murray, Mark Grey, Mike Ripka, Sam Confer, Dick Tressler, David Young.

The JV team experienced a very successful season with a record of nine wins and three losses. The young Raiders fell to Altoona (7-1); Clearfield (11-1); and Philipsburg (5-1). Victims were: Penns Valley (14-11 & 11-2); Clearfield (9-3); Philipsburg (11-1); Bald Eagle Area (12-6 & 14-7); State College (9-7 & 3-2); and Lewistown (3-2).

Coach Don Robinson submitted his annual baseball budget, which was scrutinized by the high school principal. One of the items on the budget was pine tar rags, and the principal asked Robby why he needed them. He replied, "They help players get a more adhesive grip on the bat". The principal then asked, "Whatever happened to spit and dirt?"

World Series: Pittsburgh Pirates over the Baltimore Orioles, 4-3.

College World Series Champion: Cal State-Fullerton.

Little League World Series Champion: Pu-Tzu Town, Hsien, Taiwan.

July 13—Nolan Ryan of the California Angels and Steve Renko of the Boston Red Sox take separate no-hitters into the ninth inning before they both lose their no hit bids.

1980 Bellefonte High School Varsity Baseball Team
First Row, L-R: Manager Bill Baney, Mike McCool, Bill O'Neill, Tim Wilson, Jim Scheaffer, Trainer Melody Aumiller. **Row 2:** Wes Gates, Craig Hunter, Charlie Baney, Chip Deitrich, Dave Rockey, Bill Masullo, Greg McMullen. **Row 3:** Assistant Coach Ralph Gray, Mike Surovec, Scott Witmer, Chris Burger, Ron Tressler, Dick Tressler, Armond Aquilino, Alan Luther, David Young, Coach Don Robinson.

The 1980 Red Raiders compiled a Central Penn League record of 7 wins and 7 losses; but won their last 6 games to finish at 11-10. The highlight of the season was going into the Indiana Invitational Baseball Tournament with a 7-10 record and taking first-place honors.

Bellefonte defeated Erie McDowell 5-0 with its ace Chris Burger on the mound while Indiana topped Johnstown in the other first-round game. In the finals, with Chris Burger again on the hill, the Raiders won the championship with a 9-4 win over Indiana. Burger was named the Most Valuable Player in the tournament. The Indiana coach was amazed, and stated "You guys must be in a tough league!"

Outside the tournament, the Raiders had wins over: Chief Logan (1-0); Lewistown (13-6); Penns Valley (3-2 & 4-2); Bald Eagle Nittany (10-0); Bald Eagle Area (7-1 & 4-3); Philipsburg (5-1); and Lock Haven (15-5). Losses were to: Tyrone (5-1); Altoona (4-3); State College (10-1 & 7-1); Clearfield (6-4 & 9-1); Philipsburg (7-4); Lock Haven (5-4); Bald Eagle Nittany (3-1); and Chief Logan (7-1).

The 1980 season marked the end of Coach Ralph Gray's coaching career at Bellefonte High School, ending 17 years as an assistant to Don Robinson.

Gray's son Bill was playing for the Penns Valley Varsity at the time; and he didn't want to coach against him.

133

The Red Raiders travelled to Indiana on Saturday, May 17 for an Invitational Tournament that included Johnstown, Erie McDowell, and Indiana. In spite of their losing record, they won the tournament with a great performance by Chris Burger, who pitched both games and came away with the Most Valuable Player Award.

Burger struck out 18 in a 5-0 win over Erie McDowell and came right back to beat Indiana in the title game, 9-4. He struck out five Little Indians.

Coach Don Robinson planned to use Burger for both games. The first game was scheduled for around 11 a.m., and the title game was set for about 4:30 p.m. It looked like rain, so the consolation game was moved to another field and the title game was played about 15 minutes after the McDowell game.

Burger had close to 11 days rest and got ahead of the hitters most of the time with an 0-2 count. He started to tire in the second game, but was determined to get 19 strikeouts for the day to match New York pitcher Tom Seaver. Greg McMullen called a great game behind the plate.

In seven innings against Erie McDowell, Burger pitched a 2-hitter and walked two. He struck out three batters in the second, third, fourth, and sixth; and two in the first, fifth, and seventh innings. The Tribe gave him plenty of offensive support in pounding out 10 hits. Wes Gates had three hits and Armond Aquilino had a pair, including a triple.

The Red Raiders scored two runs in the second against McDowell on Aquilino and Burger singles, a stolen base, an error, and a single by Gates.

Bill Masullo singled in a run in the fourth to make it 3-0 and two insurance runs were added in the sixth on singles by Gates, Masullo, and Bill O'Neill, and a delayed steal gave Burger a 5-0 cushion.

Indiana (20-3) beat Johnstown 9-4 to reach the finals, and in the title game went with their ace, lefty Tom McCormick, who had two no-hitters to his credit for the season, including a perfect game. His fast ball was clocked at 85 m.p.h.

The Tribe had seven hits off McCormick and three more off three relievers.

Aquilino singled in two runs in the first and two more in the third. Bellefonte added on in the seventh when O'Neill led off with a triple, and scored on a squeeze bunt by Dave Rockey. A walk to McMullen, and an Aquilino single made it 7-4. A Gates single and Al Luther's double ended the scoring for the Raiders.

Indiana loaded the bases in the bottom of the seventh, but a double play by the Raiders ended the threat.

A. Acquilino

C. Burger

C. Hunter

A. Luther

B. Masullo

B. O'Neill

J. Scheaffer

R. Tressler

T. Wilson

S. Witmer

1980 Seniors

Chris Burger

Bill O'Neill

1980 Bellefonte Junior Varsity Baseball Team

First Row, L-R: Jim Wilson, Mark Grey, Sam Confer, Mike Ripka Tom McCool. **Row 2:** Greg Gordon, Gary Catalano, Ron Surovec, Todd Clouser, Scott Taylor, Bill Baney. **Row 3:** Scott Witherite, Scott Whitehill, Jim Josefik, Jim Drapcho, Nevin Grove, Jinks Shaw. **Row 4:** Alan Bowersox, Bob Rice, Curt Moore, Scott Sharp. Missing: Mike Corbett, Doug Ishler, and Geoff Kline.

Coach Denny Leathers (at left) stated, "This was a very successful season as far as won-lost record, but more important than that, we believe we have some fine prospects that will help our varsity next season."

1981 Bellefonte High School Varsity Baseball Team
First Row, L-R: Dave Rockey, Mark Grey, Lynn Tressler, Mike Ripka. **Row 2:** Manager Jennifer Bliss, Chip Deitrich, David Young, Jinks Shaw, Mike McCool, Scott Sharpe, Dick Tressler, Manager Heather Mensch. **Row 3:** Coach Don Robinson, Charlie Baney, Sam Jones, Bob Rice, Jim Josefik, Jim Wilson, and Greg McMullen. Absent from photo: Assistant Coach Denny Leathers.

The Red Raiders completed another winning season with a record of 12-11-1 and finished third in the Indiana Invitational Baseball Tournament by topping Erie McDowell 9-3, after falling to Indiana, 5-1. However, Bellefonte finished with a 6-8 record in the Central Penn League.

1981 would mark the last season for Coach Don Robinson at the helm of the Red Raiders, as he took a sabbatical leave in the 1981-82 school year; and returned for the 1983 season as an assistant to Coach Denny Leathers. Robinson continued as Leathers' assistant for the next 18 years, thus ending his baseball coaching career at Bellefonte High School with 36 years of service.

Other victories in 1981: Lewistown (10-7); Tyrone (5-4 & 8-3); Altoona (13-4); Lock Haven (19-9 & 4-0); Penns Valley (12-8 & 11-0); Bald Eagle Nittany (2-0); Bald Eagle Area (3-0); and Chief Logan (5-2). Defeats were at the hands of: Altoona (5-4); State College (13-3 &12-4); Clearfield (3-0 & 14-8); Bald Eagle Nittany (8-5); Bald Eagle Area (15-0); and Philipsburg (4-3 & 3-2). The first game with Chief Logan ended in a 5-5 deadlock.

Bellefonte lost to State College, 9-1 in the District VI Tournament.

1981 Bellefonte High School Junior Varsity Baseball Team

First Row L-R: Manager Sandra Johnson, Toby Capparelle, Todd Smith, Mike Wert, Billy Davis, Wes Gates, Glenn Warefield, Lee McDonnell. **Row 2:** Erik Shay, Thad Eisenhower, Scott Irwin, Leo Weber, Tom McCool, Nevin Grove, Mike Corbett, Dave Brooks, Gary Catalano, Ed McGovern, Alan Bowersox, Dave Woodring, Jerry Bernhard, Tom Alterio, Coach Joe "Bucky" Quici.

The junior raiders under new coach Bucky Quici showed a lot of promise for the 1982 varsity team by finishing with an impressive 9-5 record. Two victories over arch-rival Bald Eagle Area and a 10-5 victory over State College highlighted the season.

Below: 1981 Seniors

Dick Tressler   **MVP Greg McMullen**   **Sam Jones**
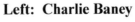
Left: Charlie Baney   **Right: Carl "Chip" Deitrich**

April 9, 1981—State College 13, Bellefonte 3. First time the Raiders lost by the 10-run rule.

April 28, 1981—First time in 5 years that Bald Eagle Coach Alex Murnyack beat Bellefonte. Score: 9-0.

138

Tom Burger

A PAIR OF ACES

Tom Burger
1972 Record: 8-0
1973 Record 9-0
Total Innings Pitched: 119
Winning pitcher three times against Philipsburg in both the 1972 and 1973 Central Penn League Championship seasons. His 17th win was in the 1973 District VI finals against Philipsburg. Bellefonte was 30-2 during his high school career.

Tom Dann
1974 Record: 1-0
1975 Record: 1-1
1976 Record: 8-4
1977 Record 14-1
BHS Records: Most wins in a season (14); most career wins (24).
Total Innings Pitched: 203.4
1976: Winning pitcher in Dist. 6 Championship Game.
1977 Statistics:
Innings Pitched 98.4; ERA: 0.85
Strikeouts 186; Hits: 42
Walks: 35; Earned Runs: 12
Strikeouts/Inning: 1.9; 2 no-hitters.
Winning Pitcher: Central Penn League Championship Game and all three District VI Playoff Games; and threw a no-hitter in the district finals against West Branch with 10 strikeouts in 5 innings.
P.I.A.A. Tournament: Beat Valley View 10-5; lost to Hatboro Horsham (eventual state champion) 3-1.

Tom Dann

Robby's 18-Year Record

Year	League Record	Overall Record	Championships
1964	8-0	9-1	Central Penn League
1965	1-7	2-8	
1966	7-3	9-4	Central Penn League
1967	8-2	8-5	Central Penn League
1968	10-0	15-1	Central Penn League; District 6
1969	6-4	10-4	
1970	6-4	7-6	
1971	5-5	6-6	
1972	12-0	13-2	Central Penn League
1973	11-1	17-1	Central Penn League; District 6
1974	8-3	12-6	
1975	8-6	9-6	
1976	10-4	14-6	District 6
1977	13-1	20-3	Central Penn League; District 6
1978	10-4	15-6	
1979	10-4	10-7	
1980	7-7	11-10	Indiana Invitational
1981	6-8	12-11-1	
18 years	146-63	199-93-1	7 Central Penn; 4 District 6

Bellefonte vs. Central Penn League Opponents:	Won	Lost	Pct.
Bellefonte vs. State College............................	23	13	.639
Bellefonte vs. Bald Eagle Area.......................	26	10	.722
Bellefonte vs. Penns Valley...........................	26	10	.722
Bellefonte vs. Philipsburg-Osceola....................	23	12	.659
Bellefonte vs. Lock Haven............................	26	6	.812
Bellefonte vs. Bald Eagle Nittany....................	12	2	.857
Bellefonte vs. Clearfield.............................	10	10	.500
	146	63	.699

Bellefonte Coaching Staff	Position	Years
Don Robinson	Head Coach	18 (1964-1981)
Ralph Gray	Assistant Coach	17 (1964-1980)
Denny Leathers	Assistant Coach	6 (1971-73; 1979-1981)

Undefeated in Central Penn League: 1964 (8-0); 1968 (10-0); 1972 (12-0).

Winning stretches: 1966-68 (32-10); 1972-73 (30-2); 1977-78 (35-9).

Bellefonte Athletics 1964-1981
Football—Boys Basketball—Wrestling—Baseball

Football

Wins	Losses	Ties	Pct.
71	102	4	.412

Basketball

Wins	Losses	Ties	Pct.
176	190	NA	.481

Wrestling

Wins	Losses	Ties	Pct.
91	152	2	.376

Baseball

Wins	Losses	Ties	Pct.
199	93	1	.681

From 1964-1981, a period of 18 years, Baseball was the only sport at Bellefonte High School with a winning record, that being close to 70%.

Epilogue

RED RAIDER BASEBALL

1964-1981

"A WINNING TRADITION"

It was my pleasure and privilege to serve as head coach of the Bellefonte Area High School Baseball Team from 1964 to 1981. Under Coach Gray, Coach Leathers, and myself the baseball program at Bellefonte High School became recognized as one of the best programs in central Pennsylvania.

During those 18 years, the Raider Baseball Teams won 199 games, lost 93, and tied 1. They captured 7 Central Penn League Titles and 4 District VI Championships. The 1977 team participated in the first State Baseball Championship and lost to eventual state champion, Hatboro-Horsham by a score of 3 to 1.

I feel the secret to the baseball team's success was the willingness to work and the PRIDE in doing a good job. Every winning baseball team was dedicated to the task of winning. It was a case of team effort, team hustle, teamwork and LOVE for the game. Everyone wanted to continue this tradition of winning. After all, why even play those games if we did not go out with the attitude that we were going to win.

When boys graduated from our program, we liked to feel that they had taken something with them besides baseball skills. They really played the game well and hopefully developed many character traits that would have strong carry-over in years to come.

I would like to thank assistant coaches Ralph Gray and Dennis Leathers for a job well done and all former Red Raider baseball players who were part of the long and proud tradition of winning baseball at Bellefonte.

Yours in Baseball,

Don Robinson

Don Robinson

William Ralph Gray

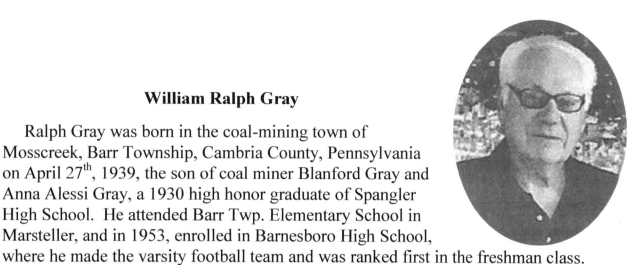

Ralph Gray was born in the coal-mining town of Mosscreek, Barr Township, Cambria County, Pennsylvania on April 27th, 1939, the son of coal miner Blanford Gray and Anna Alessi Gray, a 1930 high honor graduate of Spangler High School. He attended Barr Twp. Elementary School in Marsteller, and in 1953, enrolled in Barnesboro High School, where he made the varsity football team and was ranked first in the freshman class.

In 1954 Spangler and Barnesboro High Schools formed a jointure under the name of Northern Cambria. Ralph made the starting team as a sophomore and played three years for the Black and Gold. As a senior in 1956 he captained the team, was a nominee for the Point Stadium Award, made Johnstown High School's All-Opponent Team, and received the Joseph A. Daugherty Award as the team's most valuable player. In 1957 he graduated from the Barnesboro Unit of Northern Cambria High School.

George Washington University, in Washington, DC, was chosen by Ralph from several scholarship offers, and after one year, he transferred to Indiana State College in Indiana, Pa. After sitting out a year, he was a 2-year starter at halfback on both sides of the ball and graduated in 1961 with a B.S. Degree in Education.

He then taught mathematics at Bellefonte High for 20 years, was the Head of the Math Department, and coached high school and legion baseball in Bellefonte for 19 years. Ralph earned a M.Ed. in Mathematics from Penn State University in 1965, and in 1981 joined the staff at Penns Valley Jr.-Sr. High School where he became Math Dept. head and taught college level calculus as a certified instructor of the University of Pittsburgh. He was a P.I.A.A. football official for 30 years.

He retired in 1997, and has written articles for the Barnesboro Star, The Star Courier and Plymouth Magazine. He is the editor of the annual newsletter for the Class of 1957 of Northern Cambria, Barnesboro Unit. He compiled a yearbook for the 50th Reunion of his high school graduating class, and is the author of *The Armistice Day Classic*, a History of the Barnesboro-Spangler football rivalry; *They Came Together,* a book about the end of the rivalry and the beginning of the Northern Cambria era; *Champions Along the West Branch, Volumes I & II,* books about the championship seasons of Barnesboro, Spangler, and Northern Cambria; *A Mission in the Valley,* a History of Saint Kateri Tekakwitha Catholic Church in Penns Valley; *The Battle of Benner Pike,* a History of the Bellefonte-State College football rivalry; *The School on the Hill,* a History of the Bellefonte Academy Cougars; *The Wizard of Centre Hall,* the life and times of Vernon Hoy Garbrick; *The Buff and Blue,* a Football History of the George Washington U. Colonials; and *Little City of Black Diamonds,* a coal-mining story of yesteryear.

Acknowledgements

Bill Gray
Ron Bracken
Steve Crowley
Doug Leathers
Mike Kelleher
Harry Hunt
Jon Watson
Ken McMullen
LeDon Young
Fred Smith

Terry Glunt
Natalie Gray Burch
Jay Robinson
Dick Leathers
Joanne Rackowski Stone
Joanne Spicher Horner
Judge Charles Brown
Charlie Doland
Jeff Wert
Carl Bjalme

Don Robinson
Bill Luther
Denny Leathers
Dick Kelleher
Joe Quici
Phyllis Corman
Frank Clemson
Rod Mitchell
Marty Ilgen
John Paul Jones

Bibliography

Centre Daily Times
Tyrone Daily News
The Daily Collegian
The Altoona Mirror
The Centre Democrat
The Centre Reporter

Bellefonte H.S. Yearbooks, *LaBelle*
Centre County Historical Museum
Penn State Yearbooks, *LaVie*
Blood, Sweat, and Tears, by Harry E. Breon
The School on the Hill, by Ralph Gray
The Battle of Benner Pike, by Ralph Gray

Index

Abbott, 38, 70, 88, 96, 98, 100
Adams, 12, 25, 43, 107, 112, 113, 114, 116, 117, 121, 128
Alessi, 143
Alterio, 61, 64, 94, 103, 106, 138
Anderson, 10, 15, 17, 26, 77, 80
Antolosky, 19, 94, 103, 104, 106
Aquilino, 127, 128, 130, 133, 134
Armstrong, 67, 77, 78, 81, 83
Aumiller, 10, 11, 49, 50, 52, 58, 133
Ayres, 45
Baden, 121
Bailor, 76
Bamat, 9
Baney, 32, 48, 49, 50, 51, 53, 54, 56, 58, 59, 60, 62, 64, 65, 66, 68, 72, 73, 74, 75, 76, 129, 132, 133, 136, 137, 138
Barner, 15
Barnett, 96, 98
Barr, 143
Bartlett, 57
Bartley, 61, 65, 71
Barto, 11
Bathgate, 18, 20, 34, 35, 36, 40, 41, 44, 45, 46, 47
Beaver, 30
Bechdel, 53
Beck, 15
Bedenk, 6, 22, 23, 24, 25, 26, 27, 28, 41, 42
Beezer, 46, 49, 57, 58, 60, 61, 66, 67, 68, 69, 70, 74
Bell, 78, 83
Benford, 1, 11, 12, 13, 15, 17, 18, 20, 21, 120
Benner, 13, 108, 143, 144
Bergey, 25, 26
Bernhard, 132, 138
Bezdek, 6
Bickle, 87, 90
Bierly, 46, 66, 69, 70, 71, 72, 73, 75
Biesecker, 25, 26
Bigler, 30
Bilger, 107, 113, 114, 128
Billotte, 65
Bishop, 10
Bitner, 80
Bjalme, 144
Black, 6, 74, 143
Blaser, 72
Blazer, 69

Bliss, 137
Bolger, 125
Boling, 10
Bonneau, 113
Boone, 53
Bowersox, 36, 107, 109, 112, 114, 119, 125, 126, 128, 136, 138
Bowes, 53
Bracken, 122, 144
Breon, 13, 14, 20, 32, 59, 144
Bressler, 52
Brodkin, 25, 26, 27
Brooks, 94, 103, 104, 106, 138
Brown, 10, 30, 47, 77, 102, 105, 106, 108, 109, 111, 112, 114, 117, 118, 119, 120, 124, 144
Brungard, 68
Bugash, 9
Burch, 144
Burger, 16, 19, 34, 36, 37, 39, 40, 41, 44, 45, 46, 85, 86, 87, 88, 89, 90, 91, 92, 93, 95, 96, 98, 99, 100, 101, 127, 128, 130, 133, 134, 135, 139
Bush, 107, 112, 113, 114, 121, 128
Caba, 57
Cable, 9, 19, 80, 83, 84, 85, 86, 87, 88, 89, 90, 91, 92, 93, 95, 96, 97, 98, 99, 100, 101
Candelaria, 113
Capparelle, 138
Carlson, 34, 35
Carlton, 127
Carter, 63
Cartwright, 80
Casper, 12, 106
Catalano, 136, 138
Cathcart, 20
Ceccarelli, 124
Chadwick, 123
Chambers, 39, 52, 54, 61, 64
Christopher, 68
Church, 143
Cicci, 16
Cingle, 120
Clemson, 144
Cloninger, 51
Clouser, 136
Coakley, 12
Cobb, 4
Cobo, 110
Cocetti, 124

Collins, 120
Conaway, 16, 19, 20, 21, 34, 35, 36, 37, 38, 39, 40, 41, 43, 44, 45, 80, 151
Condo, 38, 89, 92
Confer, 10, 57, 132, 136
Corbett, 136, 138
Corman, 15, 17, 18, 132, 144
Corrigan, 105, 107
Coval, 70
Covey, 51, 91, 96, 100
Cox, 15
Crafts, 82, 84, 85, 86, 88, 95, 99, 101
Crater, 19, 20, 80, 151
Crawford, 9
Crowley, 82, 84, 94, 95, 98, 99, 101, 104, 144
Culp, 112
Cummings, 43, 44, 112
Curley, 69, 122
Curtin, 30
Dale, 1, 18, 20, 21
Dalena, 83, 85, 86, 87, 92
Danis, 50, 59
Danko, 54, 62, 63
Dann, 104, 105, 106, 107, 108, 109, 110, 111, 112, 114, 115, 116, 117, 118, 119, 120, 121, 122, 124, 125, 126, 139
Daughenbaugh, 31
Daugherty, 143
Davidson, 13, 77, 80, 81, 83, 84, 86, 103
Davis, 12, 34, 38, 62, 70, 80, 88, 91, 96, 100, 138
Dean, 10
DeArment, 88
DeCaspers, 25, 26
Deitrich, 17, 18, 19, 129, 132, 133, 137, 138
DeLong, 25
Devlin, 94
DeWitt, 49, 52, 54, 55, 57, 58, 59, 62, 66, 67, 68, 69, 70, 71, 72, 73, 74, 76, 78
Diehl, 57
Dobo, 122
Doland, 19, 20, 21, 34, 35, 36, 37, 38, 40, 41, 43, 44, 45, 144, 151
Dorman, 31, 36, 71
Dougherty, 77
Drake, 92, 99
Drapcho, 60, 69, 82, 83, 84, 86, 87, 95, 101, 103, 104, 106, 107, 109, 110, 111, 112, 113, 114, 115, 117, 120, 127, 128, 130, 131, 136
Drass, 44, 45
Drogan, 11

Dugan, 92
Durbin, 25
Dutry, 92
Ebeling, 17, 18, 19, 57, 58, 66, 67, 71, 74, 78
Eckenrode, 19
Eckersley, 127
Eckley, 46, 82, 84, 95, 96, 98, 99, 100, 101, 104
Eisenhower, 138
Ellenberger, 36
Ellis, 82
Emel, 77, 78
Emerick, 15, 17
Emery, 9, 120
Eminhizer, 15, 47
Engle, 25
Etters, 22, 34, 52, 54, 55, 61, 64, 71
Fargo, 111
Faulkner, 77, 78, 81, 94
Fedon, 63, 69, 72
Fegley, 23
Felton, 26
Fenton, 25, 26, 27
Fetterolf, 9
Fetzer, 13
Fink, 6
Fisher, 57, 103, 105
Fixter, 6
Flanagan, 111
Flemming, 92
Fletemake, 16, 20
Force, 9
Foresman, 16, 19
Forest, 9
Fortna, 6
Franco, 110
Frantz, 77, 81
Frisco, 95
Fry, 90, 93
Fulton, 11
Funk, 13
Furner, 86
Garman, 86
Gates, 10, 13, 14, 22, 129, 130, 133, 134, 138
Gehret, 82, 84, 85, 86, 87, 91, 92, 95, 96, 97, 98, 99, 100, 101
Gentzel, 20, 49, 132
Gettig, 10, 15, 17, 18, 19
Gibboney, 82, 95, 101
Gibbons, 80
Gieguez, 25, 26
Gilham, 88

Giusti, 26
Glenn, 57
Glunt, 105, 107, 109, 110, 111, 112, 114, 119,
    120, 121, 122, 124, 144
Goodhart, 9
Gordon, 11, 136
Gray, 1, 21, 33, 34, 41, 42, 44, 46, 48, 49, 56,
    57, 58, 66, 75, 77, 79, 80, 82, 84, 86, 94, 101,
    103, 105, 107, 109, 112, 113, 114, 119, 121,
    123, 127, 128, 129, 130, 133, 140, 142, 143,
    144
Grey, 57, 78, 132, 136, 137
Grieb, 19
Gross, 9
Grove, 9, 51, 136, 138
Grubb, 85, 86, 95, 96, 97, 99, 101, 112, 114
Gummo, 15
Gursky, 25, 26
Haas, 30, 39
Hackman, 90
Hall, 25
Hancock, 10
Hancuff, 109
Haney, 57, 58, 66, 67, 71, 78, 82, 84
Hanley, 53
Harper, 87
Harpster, 22
Harris, 86
Harrison, 48
Harshberger, 7
Harter, 46, 49, 58, 62, 66, 68, 71, 72, 74, 76
Hartle, 19, 105, 107
Hartman, 103
Hastings, 30
Haupt, 20
Hayes, 15, 17
Hays, 19
Hazel, 42, 80, 85, 87, 88, 89, 90, 92
Heichel, 95
Helm, 65
Herman, 8
Heverly, 73
Hibshman, 42
Hile, 80, 81, 83, 86
Hill, 15
Hinds, 34, 36, 37, 38, 40, 44, 46, 47, 49, 50, 51,
    52, 53, 54, 57, 58
Hipple, 94, 104
Hodgson, 81
Holderman, 105, 107, 109, 110, 111, 114, 115,
    116, 118

Hollobaugh, 6
Holsinger, 110
Holston, 19, 20
Holter, 91
Holtz, 75
Hoover, 12, 13, 44, 105
Horner, 144
Hosterman, 80, 83
Houser, 49, 63, 104, 105, 106, 109, 110, 111,
    112, 114, 117, 118, 119, 120, 124, 125
Howard, 9, 11, 16, 19, 20, 21, 30, 34, 35, 36, 37,
    38, 40, 43, 44, 45, 151
Howell, 56, 92
Hoy, 46, 49, 57, 80, 81, 83, 84, 86, 143
Hrabowenski, 113, 128
Hrobak, 25
Hunt, 77
Hunter, 133
Husk, 25
Ilgen, 35, 52, 144
Ireland, 87
Irwin, 138
Ishler, 49, 132, 136
Ivicic, 128, 130
Jackson, 113, 127
Jodon, 12, 13, 14, 20
Johnson, 9, 11, 20, 44, 45, 77, 78, 81, 83, 138
Johnston, 10, 49
Jonas, 25, 26
Jones, 34, 124, 137, 138
Josefik, 136, 137
Keichline, 9
Kelleher, 57, 144
Keller, 9, 10
Kelley, 6, 12, 13, 80, 82, 83, 85, 86, 92
Kellogg, 16, 19, 20, 21, 34
Kelly, 82, 84, 85, 86, 95, 101
Kennedy, 44
Kerschner, 81
Kikla, 23, 25
King, 17
Kline, 5, 10, 77, 80, 132, 136
Klinefelter, 30, 94, 103, 104
Kling, 13
Knarr, 10, 72
Knode, 72
Knoffsinger, 57, 66, 78
Koch, 123
Kochman, 24, 25, 26, 27
Kodish, 59, 61, 68, 72
Koehler, 6

Kolasa, 61, 64, 73
Kovacic, 82, 84, 95, 101
Krall., 57
Krauss, 17, 18, 19
Krebs, 80
Kresovich, 17, 18, 19, 88, 91
Kucas, 11
Kunes, 61, 64
Kustanbauter, 46, 47, 49, 50, 51, 52, 56, 58, 59,
    60, 61, 63, 64, 66
Lamb, 88, 91
Landis, 23
Lane, 10
Lansberry, 97, 111
Larimer, 18
Lawrence, 9, 19, 43
Leamer, 43, 44
Leasure, 86
Leathers, 1, 17, 19, 20, 21, 22, 30, 33, 34, 57,
    80, 83, 84, 85, 86, 87, 88, 89, 90, 91, 92, 93,
    95, 101, 120, 130, 132, 136, 137, 140, 142,
    144
Lee, 20, 34, 37, 39, 40, 41, 151
Lehman, 128
Leigley, 65
Leiter, 77, 78, 81, 83
Leitzell, 46, 49, 50, 52, 53, 54, 57, 58, 59, 60,
    61, 62, 63, 64, 65, 66, 67, 68, 69, 70, 71, 72,
    73, 74, 75, 77, 78, 81, 83, 84, 85, 86, 87, 88,
    89, 90, 91, 92, 95, 96, 97, 98, 99, 100, 101
Lennon, 48
Lidgett, 127, 129
Light, 26, 27
Lininger, 50
Liske, 26, 28
Loetiler, 6
Long, 15, 19, 21, 34, 36, 37, 38, 39, 40, 151
Longhurst, 6
Lose, 16, 19, 20, 34, 35, 36, 37, 38, 39, 40, 43,
    44, 94, 103, 104, 106, 151
Love, 112
Lowry, 49, 50, 51, 52, 53
Lucas, 10, 12, 57, 58, 66, 75, 78
Luckovich, 46, 49, 50, 56, 58, 59, 60, 63, 66, 69,
    71, 73, 75
Luse, 36, 120
Luther, 19, 77, 78, 80, 81, 83, 122, 123, 127,
    129, 130, 133, 134, 144
Lutz, 113, 114, 115, 116, 117, 118, 121, 125,
    126
Lyons, 5, 107, 109, 114, 120

Mack, 10
MacMillan, 13, 14
Malin, 6
Malone, 8
Maloy, 20, 34, 36
Mann, 105, 132
Mantle, 65
Markle, 10
Marshall, 52
Martz, 9, 10, 127, 128, 130, 131
Masullo, 11, 107, 109, 110, 112, 114, 116, 117,
    118, 119, 121, 122, 124, 125, 126, 128, 129,
    130, 133, 134
McCartney, 48, 103, 104, 106, 107, 113, 114,
    125, 126, 128
McCaslin, 84
McClellan, 17, 18, 57
McClure, 83, 85, 86, 88, 89, 90, 91, 92, 95, 96,
    97, 98, 101
McCool, 133, 136, 137, 138
McCormick, 121, 134
McCulley, 34, 46, 80
McCulloch,, 8
McDonnell, 138
McGovern, 138
McKinley, 80
McMullen, 11, 12, 13, 14, 30, 34, 50, 107, 109,
    110, 112, 114, 116, 117, 126, 128, 129, 130,
    133, 134, 137, 138, 144
McMullin, 12, 13, 14, 18, 20, 21
McMurtrie, 13, 14, 34, 94, 98, 99, 101, 103,
    104, 106
McNamee, 111
Medlar, 24, 25, 26, 65
Menna, 34, 45, 46, 47, 49, 50, 51, 52, 53, 54, 55,
    56, 58, 59, 60, 61, 62, 63, 64, 66, 68, 69
Mensch, 8, 137
Merz, 6
Miller, 6, 18, 19, 42, 49, 74, 79, 86, 88, 91, 98,
    100
Millon, 60, 62, 69, 71
Milton, 18, 120
Mitchell, 16, 19, 20, 21, 34, 144
Mock, 99
Moerschbacher, 19
Montrella, 43
Montressor, 93
Moore, 136
Moriarta, 63, 69, 72
Moses, 10
Moyer, 12

Mulfinger, 94, 103, 104
Murnyack, 116, 138
Murray, 13, 14, 129, 132
Musial, 65
Musser, 6, 94, 103, 104, 106
Nagle, 110
Nastase, 57, 58, 59, 60, 61, 62, 63, 65, 66, 68, 69, 70, 71, 72, 73, 74, 76, 78
Nellis, 11
Nelson, 107, 109, 113
Nevel, 60
Nicodemus, 10
Noe, 26
Nolan, 66, 78, 81
Norris, 56, 65, 111
O'Leary, 46, 57, 58, 59, 65, 66, 67, 68, 69, 70, 73, 74, 76
O'Neill, 127, 130, 133, 134, 135
O'Shell, 57, 66, 78, 81, 83
Oesterling, 57, 58, 78
Orwig, 75, 76, 92, 99
Osewalt, 91, 96
Packer, 30, 61
Pae, 25, 26
Palm, 6
Palmer, 125
Papabelli, 124
Paris, 26
Park, 12
Parker, 124
Partenheimer, 106, 109
Passarelli, 92
Pearce, 15
Pedrazzani, 40
Perry, 110
Perryman, 20, 34, 35, 38, 39, 43, 44, 46, 47, 49, 50, 53
Petro, 9
Phillips, 25, 26, 27, 28
Pierce, 13, 17, 18, 53
Pletcher, 10
Polka, 11
Price, 71
Probst, 68
Prohaska, 70
Pry, 111
Purnell, 58, 59, 60, 61, 62, 63, 65, 66, 67, 68, 69, 70, 71, 72, 73, 74, 75, 76, 77
Quici, 77, 78, 81, 83, 107, 138, 144
Quirk, 125
Rackowski, 144

Radick, 34
Ranio, 19
Rech, 38, 40
Rechert, 10
Reed, 6
Reese, 11, 69, 72, 128
Regel, 107, 108, 109, 110, 114, 116, 117, 118, 120, 121, 122, 124, 126, 128
Reiber, 9
Reichert, 83, 85, 86
Reinard, 46
Renko, 132
Rhoads, 81, 83, 84, 85, 86, 87, 88, 89, 90, 92, 96, 97, 98, 101, 103, 104, 106, 113, 114, 127, 130
Rhule, 31, 47, 63
Rice, 12, 136, 137
Riden, 23
Riglin, 85, 86, 95, 97, 101
Ripka, 132, 136, 137
Rishel, 78
Robbins, 113
Robinson, 1, 10, 21, 22, 23, 25, 26, 27, 28, 29, 30, 31, 32, 33, 34, 35, 37, 38, 40, 41, 42, 43, 44, 45, 46, 49, 50, 51, 52, 55, 56, 58, 59, 61, 62, 63, 66, 67, 68, 70, 72, 73, 74, 75, 76, 77, 78, 79, 80, 81, 83, 85, 86, 87, 88, 89, 92, 93, 94, 95, 97, 98, 99, 100, 101, 104, 106, 107, 108, 109, 110, 111, 112, 114, 119, 120, 122, 123, 126, 128, 130, 132, 133, 134, 137, 140, 142, 144
Robison, 12
Rockey, 58, 80, 133, 134, 137
Rodenhaver, 25
Rogers, 75, 76
Roher, 10
Roof, 75
Rose, 11
Ross, 31, 53
Runkle, 80
Ryan, 132
Salsgiver, 32, 70, 110
Sands, 125, 126
Sankey, 38, 40, 120
Sassman, 81, 83, 85, 86, 87, 88, 89, 90, 92
Saul, 25
Saxion, 12
Saylor, 82, 84, 85, 86, 87, 89, 90, 91, 93, 95, 96, 97, 98, 99, 100, 101, 104
Scheaffer, 130, 133
Schickling, 111

Schreffler, 80
Schrope, 94, 103, 104, 106
Schwartz, 15
Sciabica, 11
Seaver, 65, 82, 134
Seaward, 94, 103, 104, 106
Seitz, 18
Sellers, 11
Settle, 105, 106, 109, 110, 112, 114, 116, 117,
    118, 119, 120, 121, 122, 124, 125, 129
Shady, 59
Shaffer, 25, 78, 105, 107, 114, 116, 117, 120,
    122
Sharp, 13, 14, 15, 136
Shaw, 79, 136, 137
Shawley, 11
Shay, 138
Sheaffer, 77
Sheckler, 113
Shirey, 111
Shuey, 13, 15, 17, 18, 34, 46, 82, 84, 94, 95,
    101, 104
Shultz, 13, 14
Shutt, 6, 37
Simononis, 125
Simpson, 54, 61, 64, 70, 71, 73
Slenker, 52
Slick, 53
Smalley, 94, 103, 104, 106
Smeal, 88, 91, 103, 105
Smith, 15, 20, 29, 30, 34, 43, 46, 47, 53, 60, 72,
    90, 107, 109, 113, 114, 116, 120, 127, 128,
    130, 131, 138, 144
Snavely, 31
Snyder, 62, 71, 101
Socie, 73
Sodergren, 16, 19, 20, 21, 34
Sommer, 67
Sorrels, 60
Spanier, 26
Spearly, 47, 51, 53
Spicher, 144
Sprankle, 85, 95, 101
Stallman, 26
Stargell, 65, 127
Starr, 48
Stennett, 107
Stevens, 81
Stever, 86
Stewart, 75, 76, 87, 90, 97
Stimer, 31

Stine, 38, 70, 73, 89, 95
Stiner, 56
Stiver, 31
Stock, 4, 5
Stone, 144
Stonebraker, 52, 54
Stoner, 20, 21
Stout, 110
Stover, 9, 15, 52, 60, 64, 69, 71, 113, 127
Struble, 46, 47, 49, 50, 51, 52, 53, 54, 58, 59,
    60, 62, 63, 65, 66
Styers, 15
Surovec, 129, 132, 133, 136
Swanger, 53
Swartz, 80
Sweeny, 129, 132
Sybert, 101
Tate, 90
Taylor, 15, 28, 136
Teaman, 14
Tekely, 70, 73
Temple, 35, 37, 47
Teplica, 107
Thal, 15
Thomas, 11, 25
Thompson, 82, 84
Torsell, 11, 77, 81
Townsend, 51
Traxler, 103, 104, 106
Tressler, 13, 15, 83, 86, 128, 129, 130, 132, 133,
    137, 138
Trude, 111
Truhn, 10
Valmont, 9
Vogt, 52
Volk, 88, 91, 96
Vonada, 107, 113, 114, 116, 128
Wagner, 8, 53, 60
Walker, 14, 30, 34, 46, 47, 49, 50, 51, 52, 53,
    54, 56, 57, 58, 71
Wallace, 66, 78, 81
Warefield, 138
Warner, 9
Watkins, 69
Watson, 57, 66, 67, 68, 78, 83, 85, 86, 88, 89,
    90, 91, 92, 93, 95, 97, 98, 101, 103, 105, 106,
    109, 144, 151
Watts, 10
Weaver, 37
Weber, 17, 18, 138
Webster, 82, 84, 91, 94

Weller, 31
Werner, 26
Wert, 35, 60, 69, 86, 101, 138, 144
Wetzler, 57, 103
Wheeland, 10
White, 2, 13, 14, 15, 45, 128, 130, 131
Whitehill, 10, 12, 17, 18, 19, 20, 30, 34, 35, 36,
    38, 43, 44, 45, 46, 47, 49, 50, 51, 52, 53, 54,
    56, 58, 136
Wigfield, 88, 96
Wilkins, 17, 20, 34
Williams, 14, 43, 81, 84, 104, 106
Wilson, 17, 18, 19, 53, 113, 127, 129, 130, 133,
    136, 137
Wion, 129
Wise, 6, 92
Wiser, 71, 73
Witherite, 11, 12, 13, 29, 92, 136
Witmer, 15, 127, 129, 130, 133

Woodring, 31, 138
Wright, 132
Wyndham, 18
Yarnell, 15, 17, 34, 46, 57
Yeager, 12
Yearick, 52, 54, 55
Yecina, 52, 54
Yoder, 70, 73
Yorks, 13, 14
Young, 77, 82, 84, 85, 95, 97, 98, 132, 133, 137,
    144, 151
Zeino, 16
Zelenky, 129
Zeleznick, 11, 82, 84
Zortman, 111

1964 Bellefonte Senior Athletes: First Row, L-R: Ron Howard, Dave Long, Gary Young, Tom Crater. **Second Row:** Grant Lee, Charlie Doland, Larry Conaway, Denny Lose.

151

Made in the USA
Middletown, DE
16 July 2018